Judith & Jim's new book is really wonderful. It's filled with great wisdom about what makes romantic relationships succeed or fail—perfect for anyone who wants to love consciously.

NATHANIEL BRANDEN, PH.D.
Author of *The Six Pillars of Self-Esteem* and *The Art of Living Consciously*

A straight-talking, romantic book, *Be Loved for Who You Really Are* is a must for anyone interested in a deep and soulful relationship. Judith & Jim blend poetry and spirituality with practical, down-to-earth advice about love in its many forms and stages.

SIDRA STONE, PH.D. and HAL STONE, PH.D.
Authors of *Embracing Our Selves* and *Partnering: A New Kind of Relationship*

Judith & Jim's work is vital to creating successful relationships! The dedication, knowledge, and experience of this couple will inspire us all and give us hope in the dark times.

PAT LOVE
Author of *Hot Monogamy* and *The Truth About Love*

In their fine book, Judith & Jim share the skillful means that have made their relationship a dynamically balanced commitment to mutual healing.

STEPHEN and ONDREA LEVINE
Authors of *Embracing the Beloved: Relationship as a Path of Awakening*

This is a wonderful, inspiring book that shows you how to build and maintain a loving relationship your whole life long!

BRIAN TRACY
Author of *Eat That Frog!*

Judith & Jim have written a much needed manual for couples in a loving relationship. They've created a guidebook to help lovers through the exciting rapids and rough waters that come to all relationships. Their conception of the four passages of love is brilliant!

DR. DONALD SCHNELL and MARILYN DIAMOND
Husband-and-wife authors of *The Initiation* (Schnell) and *Fit for Life* (Diamond)

Judith & Jim offer groundbreaking guidelines so that you will KNOW when you are truly in love and what you can expect from a healthy relationship. You'll feel powerful after reading this compelling book for singles and couples of all ages!

CYNTHIA BRIAN
Author of *Be the Star You Are!*

My excitement for my marriage wouldn't have been possible without Judith & Jim helping me realize how to be the real me with the love of my life. *Be Loved for Who You Really Are* showed me the four passages of real love. It's essential for the loving marriage all of us deserve.

NICHOLAS BRENDON
Co-star of *Buffy the Vampire Slayer*

Beautifully takes the reader into regions of love we've never seen written about. Without preaching it is extremely enlightening, showing a depth of loving and living most readers will never have known before. It provides new understandings of self and others that go way beneath the surface.

MELODY STARR
Unity minister, retired

Judith & Jim's book is one that not only can men read, but they should. We strongly recommend this book because men are just as eager for romance, intimacy, and lasting marriage as are women.

TRACIE SNITKER
Director, Public Affairs, Men's Health Network

Discover how to never fail at love! You will find sensitive and practical answers here. Judith & Jim give generously of their own experience and share the stories and challenges of real people who have learned how to be loved for who they really are.

CORINNE EDWARDS
Author of *Reflections from a Woman Alone*

Be Loved for Who You Really Are is not only wise and perceptive but also delightfully practical and readable. It takes us step-by-step toward realizing the spiritual richness and depth that most people only dream about. By the gift of the authors' examples and guidance, this book helps us realize our soul's deepest longing for love.

JOHN AMODEO, PH.D.
Author of *The Authentic Heart* and *Love & Betrayal*

I've read several self-help books but this is by far the most down-to-earth and worthwhile read.

AMANDA HOYT
High school senior

BE LOVED FOR WHO YOU REALLY ARE

Be Loved for Who You Really Are

*How the Differences between Men and Women
Can Be Turned into the Source of the
Very Best Romance You'll Ever Know*

Judith Sherven, Ph.D.
James Sniechowski, Ph.D.

RENAISSANCE BOOKS
Los Angeles

Library of Congress Control Number: 2001094017
ISBN: 1-58063-206-8

10 9 8 7 6 5 4 3 2 1

Published by Renaissance Books
Distributed by St. Martin's Press
Manufactured in the United States of America
First edition

Contents

The First Passage
A GLIMPSE OF WHAT IS POSSIBLE
Two Become as One

The Second Passage
THE CLASH OF DIFFERENCES
One Becomes Two

The Third Passage
THE MAGIC OF DIFFERENCES
Two Become Three

The Fourth Passage
THE GRACE OF DEEP INTIMACY
Three Become as One

The real voyage of discovery consists not in seeking new landscapes, but in having new eyes.

—Marcel Proust

Our Appreciation . . .

The development of this book—much like any true relationship—demanded that we follow a lengthy unfolding of form and style. It even came alive under four different titles.

The richness of our understanding and the many examples included in this book would not be possible without the trust and vulnerability of the thousands of men and women, singles and couples, who have attended our workshops and trainings or sought us out for private consultation over the years.

Then there are the friends who have so generously allowed us to use their true stories without alteration and with their real names. They are living proof that we are all learning to love more and more every single day.

During the past three years of writing various drafts of this book, many people helped enhance our perspective.

Melody Starr gave us her boundless love and support right along with her notes that prevented our more academic impulses. Art Klein and Pat Feinman cheered every unconventional move we made in our style and approach and remained our safe harbor of deep friendship. Elizabeth Asunsolo went over several different drafts with the fine attention of a brilliant copyeditor and encouraged us every step of the way. Michael Hayne and Jan Landon read an early draft and helped us clarify the direction we needed to take, while Bill Sniechowski and Kelly Cline's feedback in response to reading multiple drafts enthusiastically and lovingly helped us keep our writing personal and intimate.

We also value the responses we received from other readers whose input added to the finished product: Corinne Edwards, Louise LeBrun, Rob Ruppert, Kelli Gossoo, Jeannine Lacombe, and Linda Pedrosa. And this book would never be in print if it weren't for our favorite FedEx driver, Clint Biltucci, who picked up and delivered numerous drafts of what you hold in your hands.

Arriving at the final title was a learning experience in itself and we are grateful to all of you who weighed in on the issue: Richard Hoyt and Almarene Snead, Sharon Smiley and Brad Lusk, Bryan Duggan and Karen Strakosch, Bryan Standley, Harrigan Logan, Bridget Gless, Tom Justin, Carla Becker, Terry and Evey Sherven, Nick Rath and Barb Steffin, Steve Marshall and Patty Miller-Marshall, Judith Montgomery, Ron and Susan Scolastico, Peg Green, Ric Mandelbaum, Mary Ann and Duke Stroud, Cristin Cronin, Steven Svoboda, Tress DeFiglia, Terri Casey, Davina Colvin, Laurel Moglen, Bill Cunningham, and Beth Davis.

We continue to enjoy the wonderful generosity of Erin Saxton and Peg Booth, and that of our ezine subscribers and everyone at Wisdom Media Group.

A special thank you to our agent, Jan Miller, who believed in this project right from the beginning. Our appreciation also to her wonderful associates who help us in so many ways.

Thank you so much to Michael Dougherty, director of Renaissance's marketing and publicity department, and to Lisa Lenthall whose design skill and creativity grace every page.

We are enormously pleased that it was Bill Hartley, the publisher at Renaissance Books, who joined us in the vision for this book. He and the managing editor at Renaissance, Arthur Morey, worked with us to make sure the message would gain its largest expression. Bill gave us superb editorial input that was elegant, kind, and always spot on!

Our editor, Anni Hartley, has been the godmother of this book. She kept the reader's point of view in mind at all times, and invested her superb intelligence and her passion for detail into making *Be Loved for Who You Really Are* the most readable book it could be. It has been an enviable pleasure to work with husband-and-wife duo Bill and Anni Hartley.

A Personal Note . . .

As relationship trainers and consultants who have worked with thousands and thousands of singles and couples, it has become painfully clear that while people want lifelong romance more than almost anything else, they are unable to create and enjoy it because they have no idea what to expect from love when it comes into their life. And, bottom line, that is the cause of most breakups and divorce.

While our academic and professional backgrounds are important—Judith is a clinical psychologist who was in private practice for twenty-three years; Jim has a doctorate in Human Behavior and for over ten years specialized in counseling men—it is our personal histories and the discoveries we've made together that lay the most compelling groundwork for this book.

We've been married to each other for almost fourteen years, Judith's first and Jim's third. But before we met and followed where love took us, we weren't available for real intimacy.

Judith: I didn't marry until I was forty-four and married Jim. Ever since I read *Gone with the Wind* when I was fourteen, I had been caught up in romantic fantasy, unconsciously chasing the perfect Prince Charming. Since he doesn't exist, I was depressed most of the time, frustrated with this thing everyone called love. But I never gave up.

Jim: From the time I was twenty until I was forty, I had twelve relationships including two marriages. I considered each one significant and yet could not make them last. For me, love was confusing and very painful. But I kept searching, determined to have what I intuited was possible.

In order to share and enjoy the relationship we now have, we had to overcome the limitations of our family backgrounds—both personally and as models for marriage. We had to discover and develop our ability to love and be loved for who we really are, to understand that a fulfilling relationship is co-created by two equals on the basis of trust and respect, that day-to-day intimacy is real and not merely the longing of fantasy, and that romance can be kept alive throughout the life of a marriage. None of that was provided in the families of our childhoods.

Along the way, we've charted what we call the *arc of love,* the predictable and necessary path that romantic love lays out before two people who want to build a life together.

Whenever we describe the arc of love and its unavoidable lessons to our clients and workshop participants, they routinely thank us for opening their eyes to why they've had such trouble with their relationships. And they express relief because they can see that what they hoped a relationship could be is actually possible, and it can be theirs. We later hear from many of them as they joyously share how they co-created their newfound intimacy and the blessing of daily romance.

We are going to share the same information with you so that you too can enjoy being loved for who you really are.

Be Loved for Who You Really Are is a map showing you how to discover the personal and spiritual treasure of lifelong romance. You will learn to go beneath the surface of your relationship so you can lovingly and successfully deal with all the areas of your life together. Remember, this book is just the map. The treasure waiting to be discovered, all along your journey, is the very real and lasting romance you've always wanted.

We have written this book for anyone interested in having more love in their life—from teens who are just starting out to octogenarians finding themselves in love again, whether you are single and looking, dating, going with someone, living together, or married.

Please note that throughout the book we've used the terms lover, beloved, partner, and spouse almost interchangeably.

Although our primary focus in the book is the intimate relationships between men and women, *Be Loved for Who You Really Are* is appropriate for all close personal relationships, such as friendships, parental relationships, and even long-term workplace relationships, because the dynamics are very much the same.

We dedicate this book to you for having the heart to know there is more meaning in life and love than you've understood and experienced thus far. We respect you for having the desire to learn more about the emotional expansiveness and spiritual generosity that are available only through an intimate relationship with someone who genuinely loves you for who you really are and who you love in exactly the same way.

Judith & Jim

CHAPTER ONE

Why You Can't Fail at Love

*Y*ou may know how to find her G-spot. You may know how to turn him on with the most heavenly Beef Wellington this side of the Atlantic. You may know that if what you want is a loving, trust-filled, lifelong bond, you can't follow anyone else's rules. You may even know that men and women actually come from earth, no matter how different they may be.

But, like most everyone, you keep stumbling over the same old difficulties when it comes to a long-term, committed relationship, whether in marriage or not.

Why?

When you allow love to enter your heart, it has special designs on you. It wraps itself around you and urges you to surrender to what it wants from you. That's right, what it wants *from* you.

And here you thought it was the other way around, that love would make everything right—rid you of loneliness, fulfill your fantasies. In other words, meet your every expectation, and turn your life into nonstop joy

Instead, you just keep getting hurt, confused, and even enraged by love.

Some people come to believe that there's something wrong with love. "It's a fool's dream," they mutter, "full of promise but no payoff."

Others decide there's something wrong with them. They either give up or spend years and thousands of dollars trying to make themselves right. But their lives don't change.

Well, why *doesn't* love match your expectations?

What we've discovered through our own past relationships and those of the many, many couples and singles we've worked with is that almost everyone's understanding and expectations of love and romance are incomplete. Not off the mark, for the most part, but incomplete.

One of a Kind

On this entire planet there is not nor can there be another you. That's a fact of life. You are one of a kind. Well, so is your lover. If you don't get it, really get it, that the one you are falling in love with, or the one you've been with perhaps for years, is different from you, then your relationship is incomplete and can never fulfill its promise.

Oh sure, you see the obvious differences such as height, weight, sex, taste in clothes, and so on, but we're talking about something far more than that.

When you understand, emotionally and spiritually, the very real and significant fact that the other person, your partner, is truly *other*—different and distinct from you, in a sense a whole other world—then your relationship is not only grounded in reality, but it also has its roots deep into the truth of what love can be and what the two of you can create together.

To be loved for who you really are means to be loved in your wholeness, to be loved for the one-of-a-kind that you truly are. And that is exactly what you must return to the one you love.

Bring to mind couples you know who spend their time and energy determined to change each other. You know what a mess that leads to. Yes, change is a necessary part of being in a relationship. But it's disaster when you're trying to force the other person to be what you want him or her to be, when you see the ways your partner is different from you as something that needs to be fixed. That doesn't work because it can't work. You don't really see your partner as an *other person*. You see him or her as an extension of you, whether you're aware of that or not.

And don't you resist when your partner tries to force you into a picture he or she insists on about who you should be?

The good news is, you don't have to continue that any longer.

Our clients have learned from us that their differences were not the problem. In fact, we showed them how their differences were the source of the deepest and sweetest romance and intimacy they could imagine, and how their relationships could even exceed their expectations, bringing them a depth and trust in love that they hadn't ever known. And that's what we're bringing to you in this book. So if what you want is to be loved for who you really are, please keep reading.

Success or Failure

Conventional ideas of success and failure in dating and marriage no longer work. They are, in fact, exactly the opposite of what men and women need today. The staggering divorce rate ("We have irreconcilable differences!"), the resignation that so many married couples feel ("Is this all there is?"), and the chronic grievance that single people express ("Why is it so hard to find someone?") are symptoms of our upside down and backwards ideas of success and failure in romance.

For example, a recent remake of an old idea advises women that the best way to catch a man is to always keep him guessing. That's supposed to incite his male need to be the pursuer.

So despite what she actually feels and who she actually is, a woman must play hard-to-get in order to be successful. How long must she keep manipulating herself and the man she hopes to "land"?

Well, according to the rules, only until marriage. Then she can abandon her cat-and-mouse strategy and reveal her true self. But at what price? The man she has "won" is attracted to someone she is *not!* Is that a marriage that will last? Why would he stay true to her if she's not lovable as she really is?

Besides, if she believes that men must be deceived into a relationship, can men be worthy of much respect? Of course not! So why should she want one?

The old idea further advises that for a man to succeed with a woman, he is supposed to use all of his resources to show her how special she is: place her on a pedestal, lavish her with gifts, demonstrate that he is a man who can take care of her.

So the same question can be asked of him. How long does he keep this up? The answer is the same. Until the wedding. Then he can relax and revert to his true self, whatever that is. Is that success?

No wonder so many marriages fail when they are filled with such distrust and manipulation!

Think about it. As preparation to play this game, both men and women have to believe that they aren't acceptable or attractive as they are. They are warned that if they show up as themselves and express the truth of their feelings, the details of their real lives, they'll be rejected. So, at the altar, their fear that they are unlovable is an unspoken part of their vows. And the unspoken resentment they feel at having to pretend already haunts the center of their so-called love. Their success is, in fact, a failure.

To be fair, historically such notions made sense, when the only objective of marriage was to have babies and carry on the customs of the community. But times are changing. Now the love two people share is the centerpiece of their being together. Their individual and mutual growth—emotionally, sexually, spiritually—has been added to the list of what a meaningful marriage is supposed to provide.

When the two of you know yourselves to be truly enough just as you are, charms and limitations, warts and specialness included, and you speak the truth of your experience right from the beginning, you won't have to resort to scheming and performing in the pursuit of love. So what was once considered the basis of failure—an open and honest disclosing of one's self—is now the source of your well-grounded and trustworthy success. And you're about to learn how to have it.

From Our Own Experience

Even though we've made it our life's work to understand the intricacies of love and relationship, just like you we've had to find our way through the snares and disappointments of romance and intimacy.

Judith: When I met Jim, I was forty-three. I'd been in a number of relationships, was engaged to be engaged twice, but never married because all I could imagine was becoming someone's future ex-wife. What was the point?

Jim: I'd been married twice before. The first time I was young and naive. My second marriage came apart because of my wife's allegiance to her family of origin, which created an irreconcilable breach that could not be overcome.

Judith couldn't figure out how to get into a marriage and I couldn't figure out how to make one last.

It's in the Differences

We knew we wanted our relationship to last a lifetime, and we had many long conversations over the question of why our previous relationships hadn't worked out. It became clear that each of us, and those we were with, did not know how to make the most of the differences that are a natural part of any relationship. The difference between each of our fantasies of what a relationship *should* be and the way it was in reality is just one example of the many inevitable differences between two people in every romantic relationship.

Once we clearly understood that successfully negotiating how to be together depended on a loving consciousness toward all the ways we were unique, we were both determined to change the ways we perceived and related to our differences and to open to where love wanted to lead us.

We'll show you what we discovered and continue to practice that has held true for the almost fourteen years we've been married, and our relationship keeps getting richer, more romantic, and more rewarding all the time.

About Differences

When the idea of *differences* is used in the context of someone's relationship, most people understand it as negative.

"They're having a difference of opinion" is usually an indirect way of saying that two people are in a conflict if not a fight. And, of course, "irreconcilable differences" means their marriage is on its way to divorce court.

But most differences are very positive.

Differences can be *delightful*—the way she giggles when she's excited, or how he calls her to come see the full moon; *stimulating*—how your two points of view add dimension to a discussion, keeping things fresh and alive; and *spiritually awakening*—when you stand in respect and awe of the sheer presence of your lover, and when love draws you out beyond yourselves where you experience something larger than you'd ever imagined.

Unfortunately, people now too often focus exclusively on gender differences. Although gender differences are real, they are only a small part of what you will naturally discover when you commit to being together. Most differences in personality, values, habits, interests, background, expectations, hopes, and ambitions have nothing to do with gender.

We're going to show you how the differences between you and your partner can be catalysts to spur your continuing growth so that your love will thrive. Even when your differences lead to conflicts, as they certainly will from time to time, they can function like good fertilizer—they may be messy but they nourish the life and growth of your love.

As you continually integrate your differences into your romance and connection, you will learn more about yourselves and one another, causing both of you to change. This assures that the way you live the love between you will never grow stale and empty.

Please remember that the idea of *differences* in a relationship has a broad and very rich meaning when it comes to being loved for who you really are. That will keep you open to possibilities that you might otherwise miss.

Love

As you continue reading you will not only learn to see differences between you and your mate in a new way, but you will also begin to see love in a way you probably hadn't considered before.

You may have noticed that when we refer to love, we'll often say something like "love urges you to surrender" or "open to where love wants to lead you." We describe it as though it is very much its own being. Well, it is.

If you could see love physically, you'd see it as a specific shape that reflects its own powerfully transformative qualities as well as the transformative qualities each of you brings to it. As they converge and blend, the shape that emerges expresses the wholeness that is your life together. When you let love lead you, your relationship becomes a vessel, co-created by the two of you while containing the two of you. Love then lives within each of you and at the same time encompasses both of you. It is reciprocal—mutual, shared, and joined.

You probably think of love as a feeling. Most people do. But love is more than that. It is a powerful energy. It draws you toward one another—which is the oneness you feel when you fall in love—yet it also keeps each of you distinct, so that you both preserve your own identity and personhood.

You see, true loving requires the two of you. There must be a receiver of your love who gives their love for you to receive. Love cannot live inside just you or just your partner. It is between you that your relationship lives and breathes. So it is to the relationship that you must commit, not to one another. Otherwise you risk becoming lost and accusing one another of being the cause.

Your relationship is formed by your intentions, actions, willingness, and commitment. When you surrender to love, your relationship returns wonder, inspiration, romance, challenge, and intimacy. Sometimes it goes where you want and at other times it leads you where it must. That is the magic of a loving, real-life relationship.

Love floods the space between you. It fills your hearts and minds and shapes each of you like a sculptor shapes clay. At the same time, through your personal histories and particular desires, you shape love into a unique expression of your own.

Love inspires the deepest commitment you can make to one another, yet it is powerless without your willingness to let it live between you.

Love takes you beyond who you've known yourself to be, and your world becomes much larger as you open to spiritual dimensions you've only wondered about.

But love waits to be welcomed, because it will not enter unless you are open to receive it.

We urge you to expand your vision of love to encompass its fullness—feeling, thought, action, intuition, transcendence, and mystery. We will show you how to do that so you won't short-change yourself and miss what is possible.

To help you make this necessary shift in perception, we will share with you our own experiences of love, and those of friends. You will also read about clients we've worked with privately and at our trainings and workshops, though disguised to protect their privacy. This way you can benefit from how others live their love in their very real, everyday lives.

The Four Passages of a Loving Relationship

Love changes. More important, love *must* change to stay alive. It is not a monolithic, one-time experience that stays the same forever. It is as vital and organic as any other living thing. Love grows.

It can also die. What happens depends on your understanding of love and how you relate to the specific unique and varied differences between you and your partner.

As your love changes it will foster an emotional, intellectual, and spiritual evolution in each of you and in your relationship. That evolution consists of *four passages* that we call the arc of love—to describe the changing path of your relationship over time. By this we do not mean that the arc runs from the beginning of love to the end of love. Rather, the arc encompasses four passages that lead you from the beginning to the full realization of love.

We've chosen the word *passages* because, as love grows within and between you, it requires you to face into and grow through a number of challenges. Those challenges are necessary in order for you to mature in the wisdom of love and intimacy and in the relationship you are co-creating. That not only keeps romance alive but it's also how your romance deepens, becoming ever more rich and more fun. To see each passage as a crossing-through is the best way to understand the flow of what is happening and where you are going at any time along the way.

A Caveat

Please do not misunderstand the idea of your relationship evolving over time. When we say *over time,* we do not mean as you get older. You don't have to wait for a payoff somewhere in the distant future. The rewards are continuous as you proceed all along the way.

Think of it this way. You are a prospector and you've just located a diamond mine. All indications are you've struck a very rich deposit. There are diamonds near the surface and those deep in the earth. You separate the diamonds from the surface rock and soil, then have them analyzed to find you were right. They are quite valuable, more than you'd imagined. So you set out to excavate all the treasure the mine has to offer.

The diamonds you discover as you proceed deeper into the earth, however, are even more valuable. They've undergone more heat and pressure and so they are of a higher quality. Does that mean those nearer the surface are insignificant? Hardly. They are all diamonds, varying in degrees of value. Together they make up the fabulous treasure you now possess.

A loving relationship is just like that diamond mine. It has gems at the beginning, gems in the middle, gems throughout. The more you value the love you have now, the more precious you make the deeper love when it arrives. Love will rejoice and flower the more you recognize and welcome it, and it will grow to give back more than you can now imagine.

Spiritual Purpose

A purpose is that which guides you toward something you want to attain. Rather than living your life by chance or by accident, you live with a direction, assessing what you feel and do according to your purpose.

When you have what we call a *spiritual purpose* for your relationship, that purpose directs you toward the open and honest connection that emerges when you face into and grow from the inevitable challenges of daily loving. Your connection can only occur when you are *present* in the current moment and not hiding yourself, and when you value the *reality* of what is occurring between you in each moment. As a result, you can trust that you are loved for who you really are and you then live with a sense of freedom and further openness to life. That is a deeply spiritual experience.

There is a specific spiritual purpose for each of the four passages. When you understand them, and let love take you through them, you will know how to avoid the pitfalls and misjudgments that would have led to failure.

The First Passage

One minute you are alone and looking for a partner, and the next you've fallen in love. A new life seems to have arrived on the wind and you are thrust into that time of head-over-heels perfection.

The First Passage of love we call *A Glimpse of What Is Possible,* because the beginning of love is touched by extraordinary potential. The spiritual purpose of the First Passage is to provide a glimpse into the fullness of love, to show you more than you've ever imagined. You're ecstatic, walking on cloud nine. The two of you have become as one. However, as truly delightful as that can be, the First Passage gives *only a glimpse.*

Tragically, many people become stuck in a fantasy, believing that the rapture of the First Passage is all that love is, and they insist it should be so forever and ever. But when love changes, as it must, they mistake the change as the end of love and fall into crippling discouragement. Then it only makes sense to break off their relationship and/or finally divorce. But the truth is, they have misunderstood love, setting themselves up for failure.

When the enchantment of the First Passage recedes—and it will—love is asking you not to lose heart. You must persist in your commitment to learn more about one another and allow love to take you further into yourselves and each other, into a deeper appreciation of what has brought you together. That's why you are shown a vision of what is possible—to open your imagination and keep you dedicated to achieving what you know you can have.

The Second Passage

During the Second Passage of love, *The Clash of Differences,* you and your partner must establish your own separate identities. While the sense of oneness in the First Passage is very real, your relationship cannot unfold if you are psychologically stuck together like Siamese twins. You must grow past the oneness to assure that neither of you has to give yourself up in order to have love. Love insists that you expand to co-create your relationship in a way that represents both of you. That is the spiritual purpose of the Second Passage.

You will crash into one another. It's unavoidable. And you will definitely experience friction and stress. That is essential, because *without* this spiritually inspired impulse to assert yourselves, to allow the not-so-pretty parts of yourselves and your relationship to come forth, you can never feel loved for who you really are, nor can you love your partner in the same way.

To be sure, not all couples survive *The Clash of Differences.* For example, if he wants a child and she does not, and that's final, they cannot continue together. Issues such as conflicts of religion, or where to live, how to raise girls differently from boys, different degrees of willingness to sacrifice for ambition, saving money versus spending, sexual styles, conflicts of romantic expectations, a strong loyalty to one's family of origin over the family one is creating, are among those that can lead to a breakup. However, it is not the issue that is the cause of separation but the unwillingness, refusal, or simply the inability of one or both people to reach a mutually satisfactory agreement.

Because the Second Passage is so profoundly misunderstood, it is the stopping point for many marriages, the breaking point for countless relationships, and, in most cases, the end of romance.

When you have a clear vision of the overall arc of love, you can see the Second Passage in its proper perspective. And you have a concrete method for finding out whether what you are experiencing is a mutually shared love or whether it's something else. That is the wisdom and the blessing hidden in the challenges of the Second Passage.

But there is more—so much more! And it *can* be yours.

The Third Passage

It's only recently, within the last one hundred years or so, that a relationship based on two people choosing one another solely on their attraction and love for each other has become accepted as an appropriate means for creating and conducting marriages. That is a radical shift from how relationships were formed for centuries.

When you add to that the belief that the personal growth and spiritual development of the two people involved are essential to a successful relationship and/or marriage, romance finds itself in very new psychological territory.

So it's only now that the possibilities inherent in the Third and Fourth Passages have become apparent and desirable and the chance to travel the full arc of love has become real.

As you enter the Third Passage, *The Magic of Differences,* the differences between you which in the First Passage were marvelous eccentricities and in the Second Passage became serious and painful irritations, are now the foundation of what it means to be truly loved—not for someone you are supposed to be, but for who you really are. That is the spiritual purpose of the Third Passage.

Recognizing and honoring that your partner is not you is the key to making yourselves emotionally and spiritually available, creating the opportunity for intimacy that is practical and down-to-earth. You discover the deep wisdom in your choice of one another as your differences clash and combine to make you perfectly suited to help one another heal old emotional wounds and to grow personally and spiritually. That is just part of the real, transformational magic inherent in your differences.

As your relationship becomes the vehicle through which you consciously celebrate the truth of your experience, magic happens. You are truly accepted, no masks, no games. And, after all, isn't that what you most want, to be loved for who you really are?

The Fourth Passage

Because you've both demonstrated your determination, your sincerity, and your willingness to go where love needed to take you, the Fourth Passage, *The Grace of Deep Intimacy,* opens. The thrill and passion of the First Passage returns, but this time you've earned it. It's yours through and through.

Instead of love happening *to* you, as it did at first, it now arises wholly from *within* you. Instead of looking for love, you are now a source of love, a channel through which love is expressed in the world. Your highly developed generosity of spirit makes every day of your relationship a walking meditation on the blessings of love, and you find yourselves giving back to the world in ways that reinforce the love you share.

You, your partner, and your relationship have grown into a harmonious, balanced, and promising whole, and you are a touch point for the Eternal.

A Matter of Consciousness

Relationship difficulties are always a matter of consciousness. Success at love is always up to you. To succeed, you will need:

- a clear and firm idea of what love will expect from you;

- to be who you really are, as best you can and as often as you can;

- a practical understanding of the path you are on; and

- to know that differences are inevitable and that the arc of love, with its four passages, is real.

We will take you through the four passages in depth so you can have the necessary vision and skills to be emotionally and sexually intimate in a long-term, loving relationship.

Judith: My goal is to inspire you to open yourself in a way that will allow love to bless your life far more than you've ever imagined. Once you're aware of the deep process of love, it will make sense that sometimes love isn't easy. You will also know that each of the four passages has a very important spiritual purpose for you and your relationship— whether you've been married for years, you've begun the first serious relationship of your life, or you are single and looking forward to finding someone.

Jim: My goal is to encourage and support your freedom to come alive with vitality and confidence, so that you won't be shocked even when love changes and demands that you become different. You will know that this is just another of love's gifts to you. When you are sincere about opening to love, I have no doubt that you can unburden yourself of false beliefs and discover what has held you back from the love and romance you've always wanted.

There's No Need to Fail at Love

The beauty of understanding what love requires of you means that you can never fail. That's right, *never fail*—as long as you keep the following in mind:

- If you are committed to a fantasy of how things should be, or insisting on perpetual rapture, or focusing on how it used to be—that is not love. No matter how it may feel, you are out of love and destined to frustration and hopelessness.

- Your relationship is a co-creation right from the start. Both of you as equals. Both of you contributing. Both of you valuing one another's input. Both of you open to being influenced and changed by each other. Then yours is a real partnership and love will not let you down. Rather, it will support your every effort.

- Love must take you through its four passages, and each passage has its own specific lessons, benefits, and blessings. Then, everything that arises in your relationship can be a treasure to be welcomed and taken to heart.

With spiritual purpose and love as your guide, you will know what to do by understanding where you are in the process and what is right for you and your beloved. That is the miracle, the ongoing success available when you progress through the four passages in the arc of real-life love.

The First Passage

A Glimpse of What Is Possible
Two Become as One

CHAPTER TWO

The Passion:
A Taste of Perfection

*Y*ou've fallen madly in love and are spinning with delight. Sex has never been more compelling. Your ordinary day has become a realm of wonder and awe. Life is a miracle.

You glow in the enchantment of feeling "this is it!" Merging with your beloved, you can't stop thinking about one another. The oneness is undeniable and you gladly follow your heart into an effortless, exhilarating romance with someone who just a short while ago was a perfect stranger.

You can't wait to be together and when you part your heart aches with sweet need and longing. You beam on everyone you meet. You stride with confidence and promise. You've been released to explore more of life, willing to try new things, simply because love presents the invitation. You are a burst of new-found creativity, expressing love through words, gifts, or simply by helping to fix things around your sweetheart's home.

Congratulations! You have entered the First Passage and are being given *A Glimpse of What Is Possible.*

Judith: Two months after we started seeing each other, I was preparing for a two-week spiritual retreat in the desert, which I'd scheduled before we met. Communication with the outside world wasn't allowed. So I bought six greeting cards that expressed how I would miss Jim, filled them out, and addressed and stamped them. I put Post-it notes on each of them, with mailing dates spaced out over the time I'd be gone, so my office secretary would know when to mail them. That was a huge leap, compared with who I'd been, and terrifically romantic!

Jim: Judith bent the rules by making a "necessary" dental appointment for mid-retreat Saturday so that she could join me for a company party. It was held in a brand new hotel. We had a great time dancing, and others watched. But the dance floor was slick. At one point Judith slipped and was heading to the floor face-first, arms behind her. There was no way she could have protected herself.

Without thinking I reached down with one arm, scooped her up, and spun her around. It all looked like a dance move. The moment was so spontaneous and so magical it seemed like it was being choreographed by a power larger than the two of us.

I had never known anything like that with anyone. Something incredibly special had happened, something beyond the ordinary, and I felt very humble.

Our relationship grew incrementally. After our first date, a blind date that lasted three hours, we both wanted to get to know each other better. There were no sparks or chemistry, we thought we'd be friends. Probably nothing more. It wasn't until our fourth date that we recognized the power of what was happening. Though we had an undeniable sense of how right it was to be together, each of us was amazed at how different the other was from anyone we had been with before.

Judith: I had always been attracted to guys who were a little rough-edged yet sophisticated. Sort of a cross between the Marlboro man and James Bond.

Jim: I was in the municipal banking business at the time, looking pretty straight-laced and buttoned-down.

Judith: I told him, "You don't make any sense in my life. I've never known anyone like you."

Jim: Before I met Judith, my knees buckled for dark-eyed, dark-haired, Middle Eastern–type women. Judith has blue eyes and prematurely white hair. I said, "This is so strange. You're not my type either."

Judith: And yet, no other relationship had ever made such sense to either one of us.

But along with the wonderful fear we felt, we also savored a sense of ease and comfort. Moment by moment, step by step, we forged a loving, intimate bond that continues to unfold even now, almost fifteen years later.

Sometimes two people can recognize each other in a sudden flash of attraction. Others may need time. There's no one way that love enters our lives. But when it does, it is undeniable.

Remember, you and your lover are unique in all time and you will have the realities of your own lives to address. The time line for your development will be specific to you and is entirely dependent on who you both are. Don't box yourself into insisting that things take place according to some predetermined schedule. That will distance you from the very love and intimacy you want and it will leave you stuck in your own fantasies—which, by comparison to what is possible, are very tiny indeed.

The Touch of Wonder

The thrill and excitement of the First Passage are well known. Ancient legends tell of love potions and Cupid's spells that send men and women into thrilling ecstasy and sweet agony. Movies and television take those intense feelings as the spine of their love stories. Romance novels wouldn't exist without the turbulent passions that ride roughshod over being reasonable.

What needs to be added and emphasized now is that the First Passage is, most profoundly, a time of far-reaching vision. Two people meet and the future becomes visible. They are invited to surrender their defenses and open to an experience beyond their control, an experience of love loving through them. They get to feel what it's like to love and be loved in the fullness of their being.

A couple in their forties, Tania and Larry, came to one of our workshops. She told the group, "After we'd been together about three months, I realized I'd never known such love and acceptance. At first it was a bit scary. Everything I thought I knew about love faded. It was very unsettling. Yet it was because I was unsettled, because I had been turned around, that I was available for an adventure with Larry beyond what I'd ever expected."

Larry said he relished Tania's capacity to appreciate him in so many different ways, to be curious about his work and his love of hockey and hiking in the desert. "She really wanted to get to know me, the actual me, the me I truly was. I found myself in new emotional and spiritual territory."

"And you know what?" Tania said, "It wasn't just Larry who was accepting me. I was. I was accepting me. That was really . . . oh, I don't know . . . it was neat, I guess." She laughed and everyone joined her.

The First Passage opens you to a taste of perfection, yours and that of the one you love. You see one another through a sacred looking glass and you glimpse what you can co-create together. That perfection is real, although obscured by longstanding defenses you both put up to protect yourselves.

Having fallen in love, you have entered a kind of earthly paradise in which your souls reach out and touch one another. Your everyday reality is penetrated and you behold one another beyond the material, beyond the obvious, each of you revealed in your potential wholeness.

The Soul's Message

The idea of the soul has been part of human curiosity for many centuries. While it's a word that touches us and makes sense somehow, there's not one concrete definition everyone can agree on. So, since we are going to use the word *soul,* we want you to know what we mean by it.

Our approach is very practical. If you take the time to look inside, you can sense something at the center of who you are. That something withstands all the noise of your daily activities, the emotional ups and downs, the demands others make on you, even your own hopes and expectations. It's like the foundation of a building that remains secure even though the floors above may be swaying in the force of a strong wind. When you get in touch with it, you know it's more real than anything going on around you and it's always aiming you toward wholeness.

Sometimes it fills your experience like a gut feeling, a hunch or an intuition. At other times it's a distant voice guiding you in ways you hadn't anticipated. However you experience it, it's there, within you, and undeniable. We call it your soul.

It is the seat of your keenest desire to join with another, heart to heart, wholeness to wholeness. It contains the spark of higher consciousness, that visionary power that allows you to extend beyond yourself to see your partner in his or her own uniqueness. That you both are unique is not merely a poetic image. It is as real as the air you breathe.

During your glimpse of what is possible, you become aware of your potential through the power of being loved for who you really are and loving that way in return. You are carried beyond *oughts* and *shoulds* into the wondrous exploration of what you can fully be together—like no two others in the world.

During the First Passage you are caught in an enchantment and are enthralled. It is your soul's way of persuading you to step outside of your fears and surrender to your exploration, letting love lead. The more you allow yourself to be led, the more you will experience the beauty, the rich unforgettable beauty that resides at the heart of being in love.

So it doesn't matter if we call it soul and you call it something else. The point is that your glimpse of what is possible is a call to open your consciousness to more of what life and love can be.

Don't Take It for Granted

At the outset of love you might be so captivated that you overlook the need to stay conscious. That's understandable. You just want to enjoy it. But there are three areas of early love in which most people tend to get lost. So to reap the most that love has to offer, we urge you to pay particular attention to sex, awareness, and romance.

Sex

First Passage sex is renowned for its capacity to scramble your brain and whip through your heart, leaving you breathless in its wake. It feels almost supernatural.

Unfortunately, many people confuse the intensity of passionate sex with all that love is. That leads to an extremely narrow understanding of love and it burdens sex with expectations it can never fulfill. Sex, as rapturous as it can be, is only one medium through which the soul reveals itself. A powerful medium, to be sure, but just one.

Let's clarify one thing right now. Being swept away sexually is fantastic. It offers some of the most thrilling feelings you can experience. It is a part of love that's not to be missed. Sensual, close, and breathtaking. But it's not to be mistaken as the foremost expression of love. There is far more to the arc of love, and sex will change as your relationship changes.

That's what most people fail to understand—like love, sex changes. It must. Otherwise it cannot grow as your relationship grows.

But because notions of sex have been so distorted in our culture, they can easily give lovemaking more significance than it can carry. That's when sex turns sour and the idea of making love seems like a burden.

During the First Passage, the urge to make love, to unite physically with another, swells up from deep within you, to share yourself, to be known beyond your daily masks. It is an invitation to let go of control and let life and love surge through you. There is a joining, a merging in that surrender which hints at the potential for the sacred—that which is not immediately evident, yet capable of inspiring awe and reverence.

Awareness

The more awareness you bring to the First Passage, the more you can appreciate what it has to offer, because the deepest, richest, most tender love is always accompanied by and expressed through vibrant consciousness.

But some will tell you that you can't let your head get in the way of your heart, as though your head and heart were natural enemies. Nothing could be further from the truth.

Every relationship is co-created right from the first meeting. Each of you has equal input. Or not. If, in the beginning, you don't use your head, you are likely to overlook such problems as self-centeredness, poor listening and conversation skills, alcohol and/or drug abuse, control issues and/or jealousy, and you will lose the opportunity to confront the person you are with about hurtful or off-putting behaviors and to then request or insist on change. Your silence teaches your partner that his or her behavior is perfectly okay. So you must remain aware of who you are and what you want in a partner, or your passive silence places you in grave danger of setting yourself up for failure.

You can love with all your heart, but you can't expect love to succeed if you fall asleep at the wheel. Your responsibility to love requires that you stay awake in your half of the driver's seat. It's through your awareness that you stay present in current time and avoid indulging your private worries and fantasies that have no bearing on what is going on between you.

Love succeeds to the degree that you consciously weed out all that is not loving in yourself—and invite your partner to do the same. We call it *lovework*. It is your head's contribution to the wholeness of your being together. That's why the balance of head and heart is so important. The balanced awareness of both feelings and thoughts provides the necessary groundwork for success in love.

If the one you're with refuses to change, you have not failed. You have succeeded in getting a clear awareness of the futility of going further and you can stop wasting your time. Break it off and find someone who is available to be with you in a truly loving relationship. That is a success!

When the one that you're with responds positively to your speaking up about a problem, and wants to change and grow in awareness with you, you know you've got a good match. And that's an even greater success!

Romance

It is a universal experience that the wonderful romance at the beginning of love fades, leaving both men and women confused and even embittered. So in a recent survey we conducted through our free email newsletter, *The New Intimacy*, we asked what was the single most important question our subscribers had about love and intimacy. No surprise. Their answer: How do you keep romance alive?

In order to keep romance alive, it's important to have an idea of what romance is. Otherwise, any hope of sustaining it will be hit-and-miss at best.

So, what is romance?

As with the idea of the soul, we take a practical approach.

A key feature of romantic love is that lovers experience a value in one another that goes beyond any objective assessment others see. She is the *most* beautiful woman he's ever seen. He is so much *more* thoughtful than anyone she's ever known. Lovers stand behind their perceptions even when friends and family fail to share them. In other words, they see in one another what is not immediately apparent to others.

That is what we mean when we say lovers really do see perfection in one another. They are not creating illusion. They perceive an actual ideal and it is mesmerizing.

To subscribe to *The New Intimacy* newsletter, send a blank email to: join-thenewintimacy@lists.sparklist.com.

In romantic love, you transcend your daily experience. That doesn't mean you leave the earth. Rather, your daily life is infused with value not available without the presence of love.

Colors are brighter. Sounds are sweeter. Winters lose their bite. Nights are deep and secure. You perceive one another as a miracle, and there is a magical fit.

Your life together becomes erotic. All of life becomes more sensual, more attractive.

Your energy and desire for living intensifies. You experience the fundamental connection between all living things.

You discover that your lover has entered into you, into your thoughts and imaginings, and has become a part of who you are. You bestow a special meaning upon one another, leaving room for no other romance in your hearts.

Your attraction is powerful, like magnetism. You want to be with one another and almost anything you do together can feel romantic as long as you are connected and caring. We've heard from couples that romance was in the air when they cleaned out the garage together, got lost on a road trip and saw it as an adventure, hugged one another after taking care of their sick kids, held hands at a funeral, celebrated their tax return, joined together to confront an obnoxious neighbor.

Jim: Yesterday we were in a town thirty minutes from where we live, having a quick lunch before going to the supermarket.

Judith: I finished eating before Jim, and said, "I'll go do the shopping, and you can take your time and finish reading the newspaper."

Jim: I was so touched by Judith's recognition and acceptance of how much I enjoy a leisurely read of the paper. Her gesture was so romantic, I felt appreciated and taken care of all day.

Judith: I had no idea the romantic moment I'd created until I returned and we talked about it, driving home.

Romance will change as you change. Like love, romance evolves over time. If you continue to allow it to unfold, you will not lose it. You must respect its process and progress, which will also be your own process and progress. If you try to keep it the same as it was at the beginning, you will lose it for sure.

Remember, romance can be felt in anything you do when it is based in your love and care and enjoyment of one another. That's why you can keep it alive for the lifetime you share.

Exploring
A Glimpse of What Is Possible

It is vitally important to take action to express your intentions and insights. If you don't, nothing happens.

At the end of each chapter you will find three suggestions you can use to open further to love's invitation. We call them suggestions because no one else can ever prescribe what is right for the two of you. No one. But you can use our ideas as starters from which to build your own fund of personally meaningful practices that will honor the power and beauty of your love.

1. We highly recommend a journal for each of you, no matter where you are in the evolution of your relationship. By writing about your feelings and experiences in a journal or notebook, you develop a personal, private, ongoing conversation with yourself. In it you can explore your fears, express your most cherished values, sort out what may be confusing, or celebrate when you are feeling good.

2. A ritual is something you do the same way again and again. Rituals are important because they provide a pattern through which you can express your love for one another. For example, whenever we sit down to eat, we clink our glasses as a way of saying "I'm glad to be here with you."

   Every month, on the anniversary of the day you met, celebrate yourselves. Cook a special meal, exchange inexpensive gifts, rent a movie for just the two of you. By committing to celebrating your anniversary monthly, you establish a ritual and it becomes meaningful for you both. Make the commitment to recognize and appreciate having met one another.

3. Regularly express your gratitude for each other, for having discovered the romantic connection you share. By sharing your thoughts, you will be practicing intimacy, creating trust, deepening your love, and keeping romance alive. It just takes your generosity and awareness.

CHAPTER THREE

The Purpose:
Beyond What You've Ever Known

If we were to ask you about the purpose for love, you might scratch your head and say, "What a dumb question, everyone wants to be loved." Or you might list the obvious benefits like companionship, sex, and maybe children. Or you may never have considered the idea that there is a purpose for love.

Well, there is. And during the First Passage you are invited to open yourself to a vision of love beyond what you've ever known.

An Enticement

Falling in love is such an intense experience of romantic passion, sexual desire, and sheer joy, it may be difficult to remember that it's still just the beginning. Just the appetizer. Now, the appetizer itself is delicious, but its purpose is to get the juices flowing in anticipation of what is yet to come.

Think about it. Usually you've known one another only a short time. Can you have had enough experience to appreciate the full depth and tenderness available to you? Hardly. So the First Passage is only *A Glimpse of What Is Possible,* an opening to the future that sets you on the path of developing your love for one another.

The promise of what you can have together requires that you surrender to whatever comes your way, so that, as loving partners, you learn about one another's strengths and weaknesses; expand your love to include both of you as you grow toward being a couple; and teach one another more about humor, joy, and play, and about intimate and committed sexuality.

Make no mistake about it, this glimpse is an enticement of grand proportions. You are being courted not just by your lover but also by the Universe, by God (however you think of the Larger Reality). You are being wooed to worship at the altar of love and, in that way, asked to make yourselves available to become a couple, in the deepest sense of all that can mean.

Beyond the Familiar

The call to a lifetime commitment can begin in the most unexpected ways. Oh sure, sometimes it's just a nod at a party that gets things started, but these days we hear about more and more couples meeting in ways that took them by surprise and required them to be open to a connection that ordinarily they might have missed. The greater purpose of love itself appears to need a larger tapestry of possibilities.

In the recent past, especially in the United States, even though partners could choose one another freely, good relationships were thought to be based on how much two people had in common. Very often, they would meet at church, be introduced by family members, be set up through mutual friends, or meet at events that were so familiar that neither person would ever be expected to stretch beyond who they knew themselves to be.

But now couples are finding one another in a much greater variety of ways. Very often they come from differing religions, cultures, races, socio-economic backgrounds, and there might be wide differences in age. Love appears to be doing a lot more choreographing, bringing together people who at another time might not have met.

Why is this happening? As humanity has grown in consciousness, our understanding of love has expanded enormously in both depth and diversity. It's no longer just a feeling we have for someone who is much like ourselves—no longer a narrow, largely nearsighted experience. Love's purpose is no longer to maintain the commonality of both people but rather to move them beyond what is familiar. Today intimate relationships are responsible for opening us to change, rather than keeping things the same.

We asked a few people we know if we could use the remarkable stories of how they met. They gave us permission to use their real names and the details of their meeting.

Erin and Anders

When she was eighteen, Erin saw him briefly at the salad bar in the university cafeteria. Even though she was going with someone else, she had to find out who he was. However, soon afterward he transferred to another college.

Seven years later, in the ladies' room of a popular bar after having just been stood up, and ranting and raving to her best friend about how hopeless men are, a drunken woman approached her, poked her in the shoulder, and said, "Hey, listen. I have something important to tell you." Erin tried to ignore her.

The young woman grabbed Erin's forearms, looked deep into her eyes, and said, "You're not listening and you need to hear me!"

"Okay, okay, what do you want to tell me?" Erin remembers responding with a shrug.

"You're about to meet the most amazing man. He'll be the most important man in your life." With that the woman went into an empty stall, and Erin and her friend made their way back through the crowded room.

As Erin was stepping to the right to get around someone, a man facing her stepped to his left to let her pass and ended up blocking her path. She stepped to the left, the man stepped to the right, once again directly in her path. She looked up and jokingly said, "Do you want to dance?"

When the man smiled, she was stunned. It was the guy from seven years earlier, and he was even more handsome than she remembered! His name was Anders. They talked all that night, were engaged three years later, and will soon celebrate their third wedding anniversary.

Anders is thirty-two. Erin is thirty-one. She is very social and outgoing, while he is more reserved and private. He is a physical fitness buff, and she puts her energy into work and career. She's highly intuitive and he's very analytical. They're having a wonderful time in their new house, decorating and remodeling together.

Kelly and Bill

Bill is a chiropractor and Jim's brother. We'd invited him many times to attend our weekend relationship trainings. He'd always made excuses but he finally relented, mostly to please Jim.

About fifteen minutes after we'd begun, in walked a very tall, statuesque woman. She paused for a moment, looking for a place to sit. Bill was quite taken with her and asked the woman sitting next to him to move her chair over. He then pulled an empty chair from behind him and said, "Here's one!" Kelly smiled her thanks and graciously sat down. With a Ph.D. in clinical psychology, she was there for professional reasons, eager to get more training in working with couples.

At lunch they went out with a large group and enjoyed one another's silly humor. Kelly loved Bill's spontaneity and zest for life. He loved her straightforwardness—she ate his French fries right off his plate without asking!

No one would have thought to fix them up—except themselves. Kelly is four inches taller than Bill and sixteen years younger. The only time age and height came up was when others broached the subject. It wasn't then and is not now a consideration. It didn't matter that Kelly had never been married and Bill was still painfully paying off a divorce. They found the relationship of their lives on a Saturday morning in a hotel conference room at a seminar he didn't really want to attend.

The biggest difference between them is the way they think about and approach challenges. Kelly is good at anticipating problems. Bill usually waits to see if they'll take care of themselves. Kelly likes to process verbally, on the spot. Bill tends to ruminate and come to the table with a decision. Happily married for four years, they acknowledge their differences have made them each, in their own way, wiser and stronger. As they say, "The only thing that matters is that you make magic from your differences, not that you have them."

Barb and Nick

Barb answered Nick's listing on LOVE@AOL. He asked her very intimate questions. Not "What are your favorite sexual practices?" or "How many men have you slept with?" but "Have you ever (in the past ten years) wanted an intimate (husband, lover, very close friend) to do something and not been able to ask? When you are dating someone, do you like to hold hands, walk arm-in-arm, and otherwise physically express your pleasure at being with him? Do you consider yourself good at communicating within a relationship? Can you use a conflict to grow, rather than to make each other wrong?" and "Do you think you are attractive?"

Barb was so intrigued with his bold directness that she answered immediately. That led to a phone call from Nick and a plan to have dinner. By her phone number, he knew where she lived. He said she could pick a restaurant near her because he used to live in the same town and would be able to find any of the local eateries.

She paused and said, "Oh my god, Nick. You're Miriam's husband!"

"Second husband," Nick answered. "Three years. But not anymore. We divorced."

Barb and Miriam had been neighbors up the street from one another. In all the time Nick was there, they never met!

The rest is history. Nick and Barb say they've created their relationship out of a conscious intention, one filled with love, creativity, and growth. They've lived together for three years and are now engaged.

This isn't a relationship like you've ever seen in the movies. Nick is fifty-six, has been married several times, and has thirty children—three biological, three step, six adopted, and eighteen foster children. No surprise he teaches parenting skills through the public school system. Barb is fifty-three, was divorced after twenty-four years of marriage, has three grown children, and teaches speech therapy in the public school system. Nick is super easygoing, Barb is go-go-go. She is Jewish; he used to be a Latter-Day Saint and is now a member of the Church of Religious Science.

Nick has undergone several serious eye surgeries since he and Barb met, and she has been his ever-present, helpful, and loving nurse/chauffeur. "I'm with Nick forever, no matter his eyesight." Blessedly, Nick's vision has responded very positively to the surgeries and to Barb's loving care.

How about You?

If you are single and looking, we want to help you expand your availability to chance meetings and oddball encounters. If you're in a relationship and your meeting occurred in an unusual way, please continue to be open to the power of the unexpected in your romantic journey.

This isn't to say that conventional joinings are any more or less predictable. Not at all. In fact, we're sure that if you met in a seemingly unremarkable way, there was still something about the first few days or weeks that required you to pay attention to something unusual, perhaps even mysterious at times. In any case, we're asking that you stay open to the larger invitation extended to you through your coming together.

Love is a powerful force for change. You cannot truly love and assume you will stay the same, although that's what was assumed in the past. Today, for relationships to meet the needs of both people, a new vision and new availability are required.

Trusting the Richness

How many times have you met a couple and thought, "What does she see in him?" or "How could he marry a woman like that?" You may be looking through the eyes of conventional stereotypes, while they may be involved in something far deeper.

That's one purpose for falling in love—to get us out of our narrow perceptions and to open the way for divinity to dance between our hearts.

Not Really Tragic

Peggy and Ron met when he was in the process of divorce and she was recovering from a serious car accident. He was torn between the world he'd left, which included his children and a fast-paced life in corporate sales, and a persistent need to do some kind of healing work. When they met at a fundraiser for a children's clinic, Ron was struggling with depression and financial worries. Peggy was anxious and a bit scared about returning to her work as a travel agent. Not what you'd call a recipe for success.

Still, they felt drawn to one another. Beyond small talk over wine and cheese, they discussed their mutual interests in helping children, their efforts to avoid the burnout of empty ambition, and the impressionist artists they both loved. He even trusted her with his pain at leaving his kids and the resulting depression that was making him feel old. That in turn made her feel safe enough to describe her accident and the long months of rehabilitation after the numerous corrective and plastic surgeries.

They had no interest in anyone else present and were struck by the romance of shared challenges and the intimacy of telling such personal truths. But when it was time for Peggy to leave and Ron asked to see her again, she declined. Despite the rich, personal conversation, she was afraid to get involved. The accident had left most of the right side of her body severely scarred and she feared she might be rejected when he saw it.

Nevertheless, as she drove home, Peggy knew she'd have to see him again. Ron was so open about his feelings in ways she'd never before been comfortable with. But, with him, it was somehow different. Instead of feeling put off, she wanted more. And she had his phone number in her coat pocket.

Peggy realized that Ron's freedom to talk about being depressed opened her to a new comfort with herself. Love was calling and she could not turn away. She phoned him the next day. Three months later she moved in with him, and they married fifteen happy years ago.

Given the facts of who they were when they met, would you have predicted the outcome? Most people would say no way. Yet look what happened!

Beyond Her Standards

Cynthia was a successful bookkeeper with her own stable of small-business clients. She'd been divorced for twelve years when she met Manny at a bar mitzvah for the son of a friend who was also Cynthia's client.

Cynthia was vivacious and outgoing and Manny was immediately attracted. She, however, wasn't so impressed with him, but she agreed to go to dinner the following evening.

The facts, as they came forward, made her even less interested. Manny was younger by eight years. He had just closed a landscaping business and had taken a job managing a nursery while he considered what career he might most enjoy. He was also deeply committed to a specific spiritual practice that sounded far too rigid by her standards.

Yet when he looked into her eyes and asked her about the God she believed in, she was so taken aback by his honest interest and his lack of game playing that she found herself describing her early church experience and the belief in hell and damnation and how, for years, she'd felt deeply guilty. She talked about the church she'd discovered a few years back that taught love and compassion and how she felt nourished there. He more than understood and could sincerely empathize with her.

When he explained the practices of his spiritual discipline—eating strictly vegetarian, meditating twice a day, and giving to charity every week, no matter his own financial need—she began to see how his commitment gave him a better sense of emotional security, a connection with all of life, and a peace of mind that, as she said, "passeth understanding."

Cynthia's girlfriends advised her to drop him because "he's too young," "there's no money there," or "he'll lose interest when he gets back on his feet." But each time Cynthia and Manny were together, she kept noticing the warm excitement in her body, what it felt like to be respected and valued for a sense of self that was as authentic to her as anything she knew.

That wasn't at all how Cynthia thought love would be. But she had to admit that being with Manny felt more grounded and more intense than anything she'd ever even dreamed of. Despite her initial impression and her friends' dire warnings, she had to trust what her heart and soul were telling her.

For the first seven years of their marriage, Cynthia made far more money than Manny did, but that wasn't the point. She'd already had a husband who paid all the bills, and she knew how empty it felt when there was little else to feed her soul. Manny's commitment to finding joy in his life with her, and his pursuit of a meaningful new career while he worked at the nursery, brought a new spirit of release and ease into Cynthia's life. For that she was happy to be the main breadwinner.

Manny basked in the knowledge that Cynthia loved him for who he was, and not for his paycheck. This liberation opened up new arenas of creativity and generosity. He found himself cooking more, inviting their friends over for his gourmet feasts, and he eventually discovered a new niche as a caterer.

Love Is Calling

Even if you are open to love, you can never know what it will look like when it comes calling. There are the images from Hollywood movies, the stereotypical images of what society insists you should expect, or the way your parents told you it would be. But none of that will likely be what the real stuff looks like.

Are we saying you must be devoid of any ideas or images of what your relationship will be? Of course not. But we are saying that if you allow love to lead you, it will bring the unexpected. And that's guaranteed!

You see, there is a grand undertaking at stake. In this time of expanding consciousness, when spiritual meaning is the most sought-after goal for many people, there is so much more available in the name of love. Now when love beckons, it will include personal transformation and the experience of transcendence. That's what it's like to let love live through you and through the fullness of your relationship.

A Sacred Invitation

We call the beginning of love *A Glimpse of What Is Possible.* It is a sacred invitation to go further into the heart of love.

Your glimpse is free. No charge. You are shown what the future can be and you get to live inside it for a time. That first blush may be with you for a month, six months, for some even more than a year. But it will not last. It's not supposed to. You're still new to one another and you have not yet grown yourselves into a trust-filled, devoted couple. But the potential is there.

The First Passage will give way to the next passage, opening you to deepen your trust and belief in what you have seen and know is possible.

Transcendence

Though the idea of transcendence is often used to mean something otherworldly and mystical, it also has roots in everyday experience.

In any aspect of your life, when you've reached an end point and must change, you leave behind what no longer works, incorporate new learning and new experience, and move on. There is a transition period in which you are no longer who you used to be and not quite yet who you are becoming. You may feel lost or in limbo.

But if you persist, letting go of the old and taking in the new, you will be changed. *Transcendence* is the word used to describe the whole process. It simply means crossing through, surpassing, going beyond.

No Need to Force

In the beginning, savor the potential. It is a promise of what is to come when you say yes and commit to the full arc of love. In other words, you get to glimpse the true beauty of one another as an enticement to go further, to reap the rewards that are promised. This is the preview asking you to stay for the full show. That's why you are being allowed to flirt with one another's soul. It is the Creator's way of whetting your appetite for more.

Keep in mind the diamonds we talked about in the beginning. They are the precious moments that are strewn all across the arc of love. In fact, all of your moments together are part of the treasure you are discovering as well as co-creating.

There is so much more in store for you, as long as you don't try to grab at perfection and force it to deliver what it cannot yet provide. You see, your sense of perfection is set in a context of limited knowledge, limited vulnerability, and limited commitment—

no matter how intense and serious you may know yourself to be. So if you were to demand that your idea of perfection be fulfilled, you would in fact be demanding something that is far less than it could be. Trust the process.

Exploring
A Glimpse of What Is Possible

1. When you understand that there is a purpose for your being together, and that different couples have different purposes, you gain a vision for the future that keeps you on track. It will allow you to determine, at any time, whether or not what you are thinking, feeling, or doing is in alignment with what you want together and where you want to go.

   Whether you are single, dating, engaged, or married, if you take the time to pay attention to what inspires you, what excites you, what moves you, you can put together a picture of what you need from a future or current partner to best realize what your soul wants from you in this life.

   If you are with someone now, make a pact that you'll both share your inspirations with each other. Together, build a picture of what each of you yearns for, and clarify the joint purpose within your relationship. By staying open and taking seriously what you feel, think, and intuit, you will become clear as to what the two of you are doing together. Committing to your individual and joint intentions brings a rich and ongoing freshness to the life you are co-creating. That's a success!

   Or you will realize that you have serious nonnegotiable differences and you will go your separate ways. And that's a success!

2. As we've said, there has never been and never will be another you. The same holds true for your partner. So your relationship is a channel for the expression of your distinctiveness into this world. Take the time to answer these questions:

- How is your lover unique in your life, compared with every other romantic relationship you've had?

- How is he or she different in ways you hadn't imagined before?

- In what ways does he or she, by virtue of being different, enhance, impede, inspire, constrain, strengthen, intimidate, warm, and challenge you?

Your insights will be the stuff you have to work with to realize your dreams.

3. Communication is vital. That's why we stress the importance of keeping your conversation open. Knowing what is going on for each of you is the best protection against misinterpreting one another's feelings and thoughts. As you reveal your experience, you are being intimate and you are setting the groundwork for an intimacy that will grow and support you as your relationship evolves.

At a time when it's comfy and cozy, describe your visions, your intuitions of what is possible in the future. Describe to one another the fantasies and expectations of love that you have to give up in order to fully embrace the reality of your relationship.

CHAPTER FOUR

The Problems:
Fantasy versus Love

*W*hat problems could there be when the First Passage is so sweet, so exciting, so remarkable? And, of course, most people imagine that if they find the "right" person, there won't be any problems. At least not any big, troublesome ones.

But as thrilling and enchanting as the First Passage can be, you cannot help but bring your own stuff to the beginning— fears and fantasies, false beliefs and expectations—and in doing so you get in the way of love, sometimes with devastating consequences.

You can prevent yourself from sabotaging love by remaining mindful of these significant problems that can arise during the First Passage.

The Fear of Being Fabulous

Sad to say, some of us, more than we'd like to admit, believe we don't deserve to be loved. Not surprisingly, this applies to a large number of people who are trying to improve their lives and their relationships, and they don't recognize how they are defeating their own purposes.

Many parents are so damaged by their own upbringing that some don't even realize they're passing on the abuse and negativity to their children. They don't know any better because that's how they were raised.

We now know that young children wholly take in what they are told. At three, four, and five there's no way a young mind can know that when Mommy or Daddy yells, "You're so stupid! I wish I'd never had you," it may be that Mom or Dad is overwhelmed with being a young, inexperienced parent and the child just smeared lipstick on the living room wall. As children, we assume big people know what they're talking about. We haven't developed the discriminatory power to make distinctions and so we're left to take as truth what we hear when we're put down and called names by those who claim to love us. On that basis, we form beliefs that serve as the foundation for how we view ourselves and conduct our lives.

It's also true that many people balk at the idea of parents having that kind of impact on their young children's lives. The fact remains, however, that we all make fundamental judgments about life even before we can talk. Is life safe? Does it have my best interests at heart? Am I loved? Can those around me receive my love? Those who raise us have an immense impact on how we answer those questions. Little of what we decide is conscious, but we make such judgments nonetheless. Ultimately, it's not a matter of fault but fact.

In adolescence, struggling with that unsettling change of life, feeling alienated and lost, when a parent screams, "You'll never amount to anything . . . you're a lazy, no-good bum . . . you're a good-for-nothing tramp . . ." it's irrelevant whether the child knows that his or her parents are terrified of feeling powerless about how aloof and critical their teenager has become. The message gets in anyway.

Our examples may not be familiar to you. They may even seem extreme. Or they may be extremely familiar. The point is, to the degree you took in such similarly negative beliefs about yourself, whether you're aware of them or not, when you meet someone wonderful and find yourself falling in love, you may experience a strong need to flee, to break it off without even knowing why.

This pattern is extremely common. It reveals a deep-seated self-doubt that begins to grow louder. The little voice at the back of your head starts to whisper, "Yeah, but if he really got to know me when I'm scared at night . . ." or "If she ever found out I feel insecure . . ."

The Fear of Love

Or perhaps it's that the full intensity of love is simply too much. As one of our newsletter subscribers said, "He saw beauty in me, my inner beauty. He acknowledged my own artistry. He accepted me for all my flaws! I somehow felt safe with him and could share some of my deep thoughts and written musings. Initially I felt empowered. But it wasn't long before I felt weak at the knees and ran away every time he approached."

Even though the love coming to you is real and could flourish, it begins to feel dangerous. Either you suspect it is insincere or manipulative or just false, or you chastise yourself for ever believing it was true in the first place. And then you leave, convinced you've made the right decision. Sadly, love is left behind.

Rather than challenge their fear, many people succumb. The doubt that has been with them their whole lives has the authority of truth and the power of being indisputable. They unwittingly choose it over love. Then they wonder if love really exists and, if it does, is it worth it after all?

What about you? Even in the best of circumstances, glimpsing perfection may make it seem like more than you can handle. Fear takes over and the questions begin. Is this real or am I making things up? What does she really want from me? What if he's lying to me? Have I seen too many movies?

Your fears are understandable. Little, if anything, in your life has prepared you to trust yourself when the power of love opens your heart.

Judith: I grew up in a family that looked perfect from the outside. Undivorced parents, salesperson dad, stay-at-home mom, and me and my younger brother. What no one saw was that neither of my parents could receive love—from one another or from us kids. They could only accept obedience. What they were unconsciously teaching was that to be loved meant having to match their expectations exactly. If we didn't, we would be put down and punished. Gradually, I learned to protect myself by encasing my heart behind a facade of "I'm just fine. I don't need anything. But how can I please you?"

You have your own back story. It houses all the ways you originally learned the meaning of love. If you've never looked at how you were influenced to think about love, take a minute to remember being in your family when you were a child. What was your parents' marriage like?

Did they express affection in front of you? In public? Or not. Did they laugh together, play together, enjoy life together? Or not. How did they express anger at one another? How did they fight? How did they resolve their conflicts? Or not.

In what ways did love go unexpressed in their marriage? How were passions dampened so that a deep connection was passed by in favor of surface facade? Notice how, in choosing predictability and convention, they claimed only a small space for their love to express itself.

Perhaps it's important to remember that alcohol or a mother-in-law made it a sometime threesome. Or grievances went unannounced in order to not rock the boat. None of this is meant blamefully, just factually. For you to more accurately appreciate where you came from and what you learned to call love, it's crucial to see the false ideas you accepted as true and that now keep you scared and unable to surrender.

As Good as Your Fantasy?

The First Passage of love can be ecstatic. Words like "bliss" and "incredible," "enchanted" and "rapturous" are often used to describe it. But there's another side—all that you bring from everything you've been. And, as we said, every one of us arrives at the door of love with hurts and fears, hopes, and defenses that can get in the way.

For example, even as special as the beginning of love can be, can it ever match your fantasies? Are you secretly comparing his every kiss, her every smile with your preconceived expectations?

Judith: As a defense against the pain and confusion of my family, I developed a very rich fantasy life about what the man of my dreams would be like. I took my ideas from movie or television plots and embellished them, always casting myself as the lovely young woman who is rescued by the strong, all-knowing, fabulously handsome hero. My fantasies were consoling at the time, and a safe

67

harbor given what I had to deal with. But as an adult, they stood in the way of my meeting and committing to a real, down-to-earth man.

What followed me into romance and dating was a two-headed bedevilment. On the one hand, I expected to receive very little from love, always trying to please and never wanting anyone or anything I couldn't have. But on the other hand, I was comparing the men I met with my internalized dream lover, and of course the men, no matter how terrific they may have been, always failed the test. I wasn't even aware I was doing it, so it's no wonder I didn't marry earlier. I claimed I was available for marriage, but I was horribly frustrated not knowing how to make it happen. I didn't know I was the cause of my failure.

I had to first move past my fear and free myself from this self-imposed, though unconscious, pattern of failure. Then I had to confront the impossibility of my fantasies and open myself to love with a real live man. That didn't happen overnight. But once I was clear, I was released to become available for the real thing. About a year and a half later I met Jim on a blind date and it wasn't long before we entered the First Passage of love.

No matter how extraordinary it may be, does your love really have a chance? Or will your private ghostly lover win out?

Long Legs

Max couldn't take his eyes off the dancers in Vegas or the shapely young women at the beach near where he lived. He was a fool for long legs. He completely believed his future wife would have long legs, because that's what turned him on. He'd had lots of affairs with sexy, long-legged types, to be sure, but nothing that ever led to love.

Then he met Sara on a flight to Buffalo for a winter sports equipment convention where he was to give a talk about his company's growth in Internet sales. She sat next to him. Amazingly, they were both from Seattle and she was going to the same convention as a rep for her employer's ski-equipment company. They hit it off and at the convention spent all their free time together.

Just like that, Max was falling in love. She was the most dynamic woman he'd ever met. She was bright, outgoing, athletic, fun. After the convention he knew he had to see her. They dated and it was obvious she was falling in love with him as well.

There was only one problem. She didn't have the legs. He loved being with her in every way except for her legs. No matter how close he felt to Sara, no matter how good their sex, he couldn't see himself proposing marriage. He agonized over it. But he had to have long legs.

Sara never knew that it was Max's fantasy that won out over the love they shared. Instead, when he broke up with her, he said it was because of her travel schedule. She knew that was an excuse and was left to believe there was something wrong with her.

Valentine Flowers

Geneva worked for a large advertising firm and had been telling everyone about her new guy, Jerome. The three months since she'd met him had been the best in her life. When Valentine's Day arrived she knew he'd send something wonderful to the office so she could show off how much he loved her.

But Cupid's Day passed and no gift arrived. Geneva drove home feeling destroyed. She was so enraged and disappointed that she knew she'd have to break it off. Pulling into the drive-way of her house, she was crying so hard she nearly missed seeing the large floral arrangement right there in front of her garage.

When Jerome came to take her to dinner, she couldn't con-trol herself. She started screaming at him. "How could you be so stupid? You had to know I wanted those flowers at work so my girlfriends could see them. How could you let me sit there with an empty desk while everyone else got candy and roses and teddy bears . . ." When he started to protest, she stormed into the bedroom and slammed the door.

Jerome had never seen Geneva out of control like that and he didn't like what he saw. He tried to talk with her through the door. She wouldn't answer. After knocking and pleading and being met with utter silence, he left. Later, when she called to apologize, he said he needed to be appreciated for his own brand of romantic generosity, not what she wanted to display for her girlfriends. He hung up, deeply saddened. He saw her a couple of times after that but it was obvious things had changed. She couldn't stop finding fault with him, so he broke it off.

Although here the names and details have been changed, the stories of Max and Sara, Geneva and Jerome are true. They rep-resent the countless ways men and women can be so loyal to their fantasies of love that they lose the very thing they claim to want so badly.

What about Your Fantasies?

We have said that the First Passage is *A Glimpse of What Is Possible*. As exhilarating and powerful as it can be, it is not an immersion. It's just a glimpse. Love then has to be developed.

If you are determined that your lover has to look a certain way—long legs—or if you are determined that love has to be delivered in a certain way—flowers at the office—you will be blinded to what is right in front of you and you will find yourself rejecting what love actually brings. Because a glimpse cannot compete with long-entrenched habits of mind, many men and women don't actually fail at love—they never even give love a chance.

So if you harbor specific expectations or fantasies about love that you *cannot* give up, pay attention. They are the source of what keeps you failing—not at love but at your need for the world to match your wishes.

We're not talking about the desire for a partner who is intelligent, single, healthy, employed, a solid citizen, and the like. We all have nonnegotiable requirements of that person we want to spend our life with. We're talking about an unbending need for the other person to match your internal movie, even though he or she was never given the script.

Is It Lust or Love?

One of the most profound dangers of the First Passage is that its powerful passions incite people to make rash sexual decisions out of swept-away giddiness. They have sex and they ask about birth control after the fact, only to discover—oops—there wasn't any. Or they find out relevant details of each other's sexual history months later, and—oops—there's a threat of AIDS. Or they stopped just short of intercourse because they believed only intercourse is truly sex, and then—oops—reputations are smeared and trust is violated. Or she thought sex meant marriage and he thought sex meant sex. Oops.

We're not preaching abstinence. That's not the point. We are suggesting that the heat at the beginning of love can go hand in hand with wisdom when you remember that you're just at the beginning. There's so much more. No need to rush into bed, and certainly not without a few serious conversations about the kinds of issues we mention above. Then, while your exuberant sexual desire that longs to make its way to bed has to wait a bit, you are opened to a kind of intimate and romantic discovery you hadn't expected or imagined.

Yes, there are some couples who have sex on the first date, move in together after a week, and get married in a month. Some of them make it and have truly great relationships. But they are rare. Most often, decisions made under the spell of fiery pleasure and passion lead only to heartbreak, and disillusionment with love and marriage.

Misconceptions about Love

Because you've not really known what to expect from love, there are many blind alleys that can entrap and destroy the love you think you will have forever. Use the following examples to spark your awareness of misconceptions you may hold about yourself, your lover, or love itself that interfere with the honest, flowing give-and-take of a real-life relationship.

It Will Never Change

Because of the intensity of the First Passage, you may have decided that your lover is your soul mate and your relationship will never change. But that is impossible. Love grows and you have to grow with it. Love is a living energy. You must yield to love—not the other way around.

It's Effortless

If you believe that love is and should remain effortless, you cut yourself out of the picture and remain a child for whom everything will be provided. Love requires conscious and steady care and attention. If you want love, you must participate.

Playing Games

You can't play games with love. It will not be trivialized and disrespected. You are given the First Passage vision to introduce you to what a stable, secure relationship can be and what you have to do to attain it. But because of all the games prompted by the enormous insecurity within and between men and women, for too many couples the four passages in the arc of love never unfold. They are preempted by the guaranteed failure of their masquerades.

Pretending You're Alike

Love can only show up for a real self. Period. That's why we emphasize the importance of respecting the differences between you, for only that can pave the way for the deepest love possible.

If you're pretending to be someone you're not, you will not only miss out on the kind of love that would be meaningful to you, but you'll remain alone with your puppet self that no longer has an audience.

Sentimentality

It's so easy to fall in love with the idea of being in love. We become involved with our images of the other person and our notions of what we believe our relationship should be, rather than the reality of what's going on. We are caught up inside our own heads, manufacturing emotions that are often very intense but have little, if any, connection with the one we say is so wonderful.

When Mary Beth met Richard, she knew she'd finally found the relationship she was looking for. At least, that's how she described it when she called in to talk with us when we were on a late-night radio show. She went on to say that she gave Richard the key to her place on their second date, had a formal photo portrait taken on the first-month anniversary of their meeting, and lavished him with gifts.

Mary Beth was in heaven, until Richard suddenly announced that he felt hemmed in by Mary Beth's attentions and possessiveness, and broke it off. Mary Beth was shocked and devastated.

Those who are in love with love are trapped in a pattern of failure. Why? Because they are involved solely with themselves.

Please Let Love Lead

When love comes to call on you, it wants to be valued and received. It wants to be an honored guest in your life. After all, you've been saying you want to know the joy of real romance. You want to be married and know the depth of a long-term commitment. You want to grow together, in grace and well-being. That's what you say.

So what if love accepts your invitation and wholeheartedly shows up? Will you?

Imagine that *you* are Love and you've been invited to a fabulous feast. You arrive all dressed up, because this is a very special occasion. You bring expensive, chilled champagne in a sterling silver bucket, two dozen red roses, and a gourmet confection for dessert. This is an event in honor of you—Love!

You knock and are greeted at the door, not by someone dressed to receive you but by the neighbor's ten-year-old kid. He says your hostess is out walking the dog, but you can come in. The kid has done his job and leaves. You look around. The house is disordered and no dinner feast is visible.

As you're about to leave, deciding the invitation must have come from someone else, the hostess shows up with the dog, gasping for breath. "Oh, I'm . . . so glad I . . . here, won't you sit down? I'm so sorry . . . I had a problem . . . my god, you're so fancy . . . ummm, well, I'll call for Chinese, how would that be? You see, I didn't really believe you'd show up . . . uh, rather, I mean . . . well, here you are . . . gosh . . . I guess I expected you to know I wanted someone who would be more casual. Sheesh, you brought all this stuff for me . . . you didn't have to . . . I mean, I wish you hadn't . . . this is a joke, right? I mean, no one acts like you do . . . right . . . it's a big joke . . . on me . . . yes?"

You realize you're not wanted so you respectfully take your leave. As you make your way down the path, you hear behind you a pitiful wail. "I wasn't expecting . . . I didn't understand. . . Come baaack. Pleeease come baaaack!!"

So welcome love and let it lead, because it will never stay where it is not received. It can't.

Exploring
A Glimpse of What Is Possible

1. The intensity of loving feelings can be frightening. Your focus has been captured. Your thoughts are filled with the

marvelous new person in your life. You're on a ride of mood swings that take you from shy and awkward to more bold than you've ever been. You are thrilled with the passion, but sometimes it feels like you're under the influence of a high-octane hormonal cocktail over which you have no control.

Write in your journal anything and everything you can think of that relates to your fear of being intensely loved. Do this even if you've been married for a long time.

Make a promise to each other that whenever either of you is feeling uncertain, you will make it a point to speak up. Begin by telling your partner that you are feeling shaky or scared. That is the signal that calls for care and compassion and the freedom to say whatever you need to say, even if it doesn't make sense. Whichever one of you is listening does not try to fix things, does not try to "help" by being analytical. You only listen. This is about being an open-hearted ally, reassuring and comforting about how unsettling new love can be. Your ability to give and receive compassion will reinforce the romance between you and establish a trust for it to continue.

2. What does sex and lovemaking mean to each of you? Before consummating your relationship, please don't hesitate to make each other aware of your expectations—for example, are you expecting it will deepen the relationship or do you just want a good time? Being shocked or disappointed sexually can be devastating. That need not be if you both make your expectations clear.

It has become crucial to take preventative measures against sexually transmitted diseases. It may be uncomfortable to talk about this, but your health and even your life may be at stake. Cover the basics: sexually transmitted diseases, AIDS testing, birth control, and any other concerns you may have. Please don't confuse lust with love.

3. Search back through your upbringing, friendships, and previous dating and/or marital experiences for the outmoded, undermining, or destructive prohibitions, injunctions, and beliefs you've carried that now must be changed in order to avoid sabotaging the love that beckons you. Write them out in your journal and discuss them with your partner to gain support for working against these old convictions and false expectations.

CHAPTER FIVE

The Principles:
It's Always Co-Created

*F*alling in love and crossing through the First Passage can be difficult. Fortunately there are principles that can guide your choices and behavior so that you can avoid pretend romance and fantasy love and be as available for the real thing as possible.

A principle is a belief or conviction, conscious or not, that determines your attitudes, feelings, and behaviors. The way you act, the judgments you make, the hopes you imagine, all flow from one or more principles that provide the structure for how you organize your life. When you don't have a clear understanding of what you believe about love and relationship, you can feel lost much of the time.

If you want a love that is both lasting and fulfilling, follow these First Passage principles to help you create a deep, intimate, and spiritually rewarding relationship.

Co-Created Means Equal Input

From the very first minute you meet, you begin teaching each other who you are. What you want or don't. What you'll accept or won't. What you're interested in or not. This happens consciously or unconsciously, directly or indirectly. And each of you has equal input as to how the relationship takes form and expression. This fact is so often misunderstood, it bears repeating: *Each of you has equal input on how the relationship takes form and expression.* You are not powerless, regardless of how it may feel.

Marsha and Stan had been married for eight years. He was a plant foreman for a tire manufacturing company. She kept house and raised their two children. They had adopted their gender stereotypes without question. When they came to us, he was fed up with his work and she felt imprisoned in the house, and they were blaming each other.

"He thinks all I'm good for is cleaning, washing, and cooking."

"When did I say that? When?"

"Never. Okay. Never. But I can feel it from you."

"It doesn't matter what I say. You can feel it, so that must be the way it is, huh?"

But they hadn't always been at each other. To their friends they seemed like a normal couple. And given the area in which they lived, they were. He did the man things. She did the woman things, just like everybody else in the neighborhood.

"I'm feelin' suffocated, ya know?" Stan was weary. "I go to this damn job every day and come home to . . ." He turned to Marsha. "When did it go bad? For you, I mean. What did I do?" His openness and vulnerability filled the room. Marsha softened.

"He was the man, ya know," Marsha said. "I was raised to listen. I never said nothin'. I did what he said."

"How many times did I ask for your opinion? Huh?" Stan sighed. "You left it to me. So I did what I thought was best. Now she tells me I act like her boss. I can't win no way."

We were able to show them how they were collaborators in the disappointment and repression they were feeling. It was more difficult with Marsha because, on the surface, it appeared that she was powerless. But every time she deferred to Stan she was unwittingly teaching him to take charge. When he did, he unknowingly affirmed her choice to submit. They were a team, right from the start, stuck in the ways they were raised to believe men and women were *supposed* to behave.

As your relationship evolves, at times you are either actively influential—suggesting, requesting, pretending, planning, negating, and initiating behaviors and activities—or, at other times, you are passive—going along, putting up with, perhaps pouting and hiding your feelings. Whichever approach you take, you are as powerful as your partner in influencing your relationship, for better or worse.

If, for example, you are in a love affair with someone who is not emotionally available, and you accept the status quo, you are teaching this person that he or she doesn't have to participate. You are giving them permission to be remote and disinterested. Even if you plead, complain, seduce, argue, storm out, and then feel like a victim, those are just the behaviors that fit the scene you are playing. Because you are not really serious about change, you are letting it be known—"I accept this, no matter what I say or feel."

Your co-conspirator is teaching you that he or she is willing to put up with your drama, calling you needy or overbearing, perhaps threatening to leave, then not leaving. You both may feel put upon or unloved, but you stay together and go on.

As long as you continue this way of relating, you are not present to the reality of what you are doing. You are caught in a fantasy, dedicated to *striving* for connection. That's what you're serious about. Striving and failing. You are equal partners in the co-creation and you've been so from the first moment.

Is this love? No, although it is what many people call love.

As we said, two people are always teaching each other what they want and what they will accept. Don't pretend you are without input. That fallacy can make your relationship a misery.

Heaven and Earth

During the First Passage in the arc of love, you will encounter the sometimes confusing duality of living in two worlds, Heaven and Earth, at the same time.

On the one hand, you are swept into a miraculous experience, lifted beyond ordinary awareness. Through heavenly eyes you see beyond your lover's limitations. Shortcomings go overlooked, almost undetected. Instead, with the vision of what is possible open before you, the promise of what you can be together becomes the foundation of your future.

On the other hand, you also know you are a creature of this earth. Life is still going on as usual. You have to go to work, pay the bills, and empty the trash. All of your experience takes place within a flesh-and-blood body. It cannot happen otherwise. The pleasure and pain of existence still remain, except that now a greater purpose has been revealed to you.

As you move through the First Passage, you are able to see the dignity of both the transcendent and the mundane—the elegance of your joining together in the relationship you are co-creating.

The Unknown

The First Passage is more than just a beginning in time. It is an entrance into the unknown. But don't let the word *unknown* scare you. Every learning experience takes you into unknown territory. You venture into it every day when you're confronted with something you've not experienced before and have to find your way. New love is always an adventure into discovery, into the unknown.

When you've met someone you hadn't known before, or even if you had, and you begin to build an intimacy together, there will be much you do not know about each other. That's just a fact of life. No matter how much you may have in common, building a relationship calls for you to stretch beyond the familiar. Some part of your relationship must surprise you, otherwise you merely re-create with a new person what you've done before with others. That is not intimacy. That's a rut.

The development of your new life together will contain both predictability and mystery. You are called to give yourself to it, to both lead and follow, to control and surrender, to direct and discover it as you go along.

You Have a Choice

No matter your age, at the outset of the arc you are at a crossroads. You can reject the mystery and choose the past, remaining who you already are, or you can choose the mystery and venture into the unknown, becoming someone you have yet to become.

Dan had fallen head-over-heels for Marisca, a former go-go dancer turned veterinarian's assistant. From his point of view, she was drop-dead gorgeous with a figure that wouldn't quit. And she was bright and compassionate.

Marisca was impressed with Dan's sense of courage in the brokerage business—riding the ups and downs of the stock market and catering to his demanding clients.

Each had suffered through a disastrous marriage, and now, after six months together, they were ready to make plans for a wedding. Or so they thought, until Dan's mother came to visit.

That first day, when Marisca came home from work, she was horrified to find their house had been rearranged. Even the kitchen was reorganized. This was not the home she and Dan had created, but the home his mother insisted "looked and functioned best."

Marisca waited for Dan to arrive and took him aside, pointing out his mother's invasion. She asked him to speak to her immediately. His mother had to know she was only a guest and could not touch their furnishings and personal belongings.

Then came a further shock. Dan was outraged. "Just humor her, for crying out loud! She's an old lady and she means well. Act like a grownup, not a pouty child."

Marisca could not compete with Dan's unconscious and unbending loyalty to his mother. Dan had made a choice, no matter how he protested otherwise. He chose his past, and the beginning of their love remained just that—the beginning. Dan was mother-bound and a future with Marisca was not available to him.

Allowing Someone Else In

As obvious as it may seem, the First Passage is a time of letting someone else in. Not just into your life, but also into your being. You and your lover become entwined so that each of you is changed by the presence of the other. This is not a superficial change. It will affect the way you view the world, what you want for your future, how you imagine attaining your desires, who you've known yourself to be. These are significant changes—changes at the level of your identity.

Judith: About three months after we started seeing one another, I had an epiphany. Jim had just left my condo after a lovely dinner out and I was standing in my kitchen, wrapped in the glow of the evening. Suddenly I knew I had to choose, in that very moment, whether to allow him in further or to leave. It was utterly clear. If I continued to see him, I would have to open all the way and that meant I was in for life—with no guarantee of where it would lead.

Jim was not a wealthy man. Furthermore, he wasn't even solidly committed to his work as a budding investment banker. Conventional wisdom would have said, "Stop now. Get out." But instead I committed to the mysterious invitation that his remarkable presence had extended—well before the marriage proposal that came more than a month later.

Jim: For the first two years of our relationship, I worked as an investment banker. Judith helped me see how wrong that was for my talents and inclinations. I was impressed with her insight and began to follow my determination to work with men, offering workshops, men's groups, and retreats along with the relationship work we were already doing together. Finally, I quit my corporate job to work full-time for our company, The Magic of Differences.

Judith has become so much a part of me. She's influenced me at levels that, after almost fifteen years, I'm only now beginning to comprehend.

Letting someone in isn't so much about sex and paying the bills or even having children, as it is about joining your lives together, spirit and soul. The paradox is that, in such a connection, there is no danger of losing yourself. Rather, it has to do with gaining more of yourself than you've ever known, and you do that with and through the other person.

Everyone Is a Learner

Nothing is born fully developed. Everything starts at the beginning. And the same is true with love, although at the outset love surely feels like it has dropped from heaven, with all the completeness that suggests. But remember, love begins as a glimpse that must be nurtured and grown.

You weren't born with built-in skills for long-lasting, romantic love. They have to be learned. If they didn't exist in your parents' marriage or somewhere in your family, if you didn't develop the roots of passionate intimacy from how you were loved, then your capacity to recognize, give, and receive love will be limited. And not *may* be limited, but *will* be limited.

However, you can learn now, as long as you're aware of— and are willing to respect and consciously travel through—the arc of love.

Why do we say consciously? Because unless you stay awake and aware of your own feelings, thoughts, and behaviors, you can easily drift back into unconscious beliefs and patterns that will cause you to veer away from love and toward unloving, perhaps even abusive, people. And that will feel very familiar and comfortable—because it will *be* familiar and comfortable. But in this case familiarity breeds the lack of love. That's not a failure at love. Rather, it's a success at remaining loyal to the unloving ways of your upbringing.

Some aspects of the four passages, however, are *not* going to be familiar, because your soul has bigger designs for you than you do. As you accept the invitation to co-create a spiritually transformative relationship, whether it's with your current partner or someone you've not yet met, you will be required to develop new consciousness and a new appreciation of what it means to be a loving human being.

Compassion

The passions of the First Passage are so compelling, it's hard sometimes to remember that they belong to two mortal beings. But they do, and the intensity of your experience can trigger insecurities. Why? Because no one arrives at love's door unscathed by the hard knocks of life. No one. So it's important to remember that you are not alone in your feelings. Compassion for yourself and your lover, right from the start, establishes trust that creates a bond, securing your relationship at its foundation.

We're all learning how to love better, all struggling to follow the call of our souls to become fully loving beings. It is abusive to expect yourself and/or your partner to know in advance how to be openhearted and romantic.

When you truly grasp that we are all in this together, unfinished in our capacity to be spiritual lovers, you can relax and be more of who you are and accept your lover for the truth of who he or she is. You can then compassionately embrace the full experience, including any fear or discomfort you may share, because you will know that's also part of spiritually grounded loving.

Exploring
A Glimpse of What Is Possible

1. Because it can be difficult to keep in mind that love lives in two worlds, the transcendent and the mundane, sometimes

even the simplest reminder can be very helpful. Find pictures that represent your understanding of how love lives in your daily world.

Make a collage on a big poster board. Tape on magazine cutouts, photos, drawings, cartoons, whatever expresses what heaven and earth mean to you. Keep it in a place that is personal and private.

As your insight into the First Passage grows, each of you can add and take away pieces, revealing your view of what is happening. That in itself, even without any discussion, will be a method for developing and deepening the intimacy between you. It can be a sometimes humorous, sometimes serious, but always a very romantic project.

2. To be sincere about love, you have to admit that the unknown is a natural and vital part of the experience. It is the mystery that keeps you interested, keeps you exploring, and keeps you alert.

   There are two kinds of mystery: one is the kind that has an explanation, like finding out whodunit in a mystery novel, and then there's the kind that goes beyond words. Again, two worlds—the mundane and the transcendent.

   Writing poetry is a very fruitful way to explore the mystery of your experience together—poetry that no one but the two of you will ever see, so you don't have to worry about what you write. The point is to express those feelings that are so wonderful yet so elusive and then share them with one another.

3. No matter the age of your relationship, take a long look at how each of you plays out your half of the design and structure of the relationship. You may want to write about this in your journal.

And certainly talk with one another about how you see your own impact and that of your partner. As you talk about what you're noticing, you may find that you disagree in certain respects.

If so, just remember that there's no "right" or "wrong" perspective here—simply awareness. Your disagreements can be very enlightening when you approach one another with genuine curiosity.

CHAPTER SIX

The Payoff:
You Know You Are Lovable

*Y*ou've committed to the passion and the beauty of the First Passage. You're having the time of your life and you've never felt more joy and pleasure at just being yourself. You're discovering and understanding the greater spiritual purpose for this time of love and relationship, and the two of you are looking forward to moving into the changes of what is yet to come.

Letting love work on you can have an even greater payoff when you allow your world view to be transformed. It's not just the fun and thrill of loving and being loved, it's also opening to the new consciousness of who you know yourself to be.

Love Is Real and Meaningful

We live in a society that is often jaded and cynical. Ugly divorces, violent breakups, and meaningless dating taint our ideas about the possibility of love. Yet here you are experiencing *A Glimpse of What Is Possible,* a love that would transform the world into a paradise if everyone could feel what you're feeling. And it's real. Very, very real.

Whatever awaits you in the future, the love you are experiencing right now is so powerful that it leaves you breathless as you are inspired to see beyond the ordinary fears and judgments that usually separate people. You are given this life-altering insight into the larger dimensions of love—far larger than anything depicted and displayed in romantic movies or romance novels, which seem fluffy and thin by comparison. This love holds the world, and you are at the center of it.

You can trust that love is real. What it takes to make it last, you don't know. But that's not yet your concern. As you see the power of love transform your experience of yourself, your beloved, and even the world, you see the deepest spiritual meaning in the injunction to "love one another." You now know why the sanctity of love needs to be celebrated and acclaimed, and that is what the spiritually based vision of the First Passage of love provides.

You Know You Are Lovable

You are being shown the truth that you are lovable. When your lover compliments you, tells you that you are adored, and calls you "darling," there is a ring of truth that lets you take it in and receive it. Inner voices may quarrel about it later, but for now there is a wisdom in command, directing your attention toward you, your lover, and what you are building together.

Can you believe you are lovable and sustain that belief over the long haul? That remains to be seen. Will your partner be able to love you through the bad times as well as the good? That, too, awaits the further development of your particular relationship. But for now you know what it feels like to be wanted, admired, and enjoyed. You know you deserve to be wanted, admired, and enjoyed. And you know the pleasure and poignancy of wanting, admiring, and enjoying your partner.

What will you have to do to make this all a permanent part of your self-image? That will be revealed in due time. But right now, you know you are lovable.

The Future Is Opened to You

Not only do you see your own life differently, but you also begin to see how all of life could be different if love were at the center of human consciousness. In everyday reality, such an idea is considered naive, a childlike concept of those lost in wishful dreaming. But from the vantage point of *A Glimpse of What Is Possible,* it is merely an accurate reading of the possible waiting to catch fire.

You are, at least for now, in touch with that fire. When you say yes, you know you are signing on to become a spiritual leader by virtue of how you will live your life. No need to jump on stage, or write books, or go protesting in the nation's capital. All you have to do is stay true to the vision revealed to you and you will be the living embodiment of your leadership.

A Vision of the Eternal

Life as you've known it is suddenly obscured by the magnitude of what you can now see, and it's not just all those wild, wonderful feelings that seem to come out of nowhere. It's also the knowledge that if this heightened, glorified love is coming from a new realm, far beyond what you've ever known before, then what else may be possible?

By committing to the First Passage, you have accepted a vision of yourself that no longer struggles with the confinements of your previous reality. Love has tapped into your higher consciousness and wants to set you free.

You're at a threshold. Do you cling in fear to the certainty that life can never be this good and turn back as the Second Passage opens its doors to you? Or do you claim the opportunity to live a life of loving and being loved? Do you step further into love's invitation or do you back away?

You've seen the realm of consciousness that is not barricaded by *ought to, supposed to,* and *should,* and it beckons your attendance. As you say yes, love will bless you with an experience that truly does pass all ordinary understanding.

Exploring
A Glimpse of What Is Possible

1. As simple as it may sound, most couples do not make a practice of telling each other what they love about one another. What they often say is something like, "I love you because I feel good around you." If you say that, you are talking about yourself, not about your partner. So it is critical that you both practice being specific about what you love in each other. For example, "I love your emotional courage," or "I love your sense of humor," or "I love the way your nose wrinkles when you're thinking."

   When we do this exercise in our workshops, we give each partner five minutes to speak while the other only listens. Those who speak are stunned by how quickly they run out of things to say, even when they are brimming with affection. When you master this technique, you will not only delight your partner but you will also become more aware of your own loving experience.

2. There is the other side to the experience above. When your partner is telling you what he or she loves about you, you

have to receive what you are told. That, too, is not as easy as it sounds.

Many people shy away from being told how wonderful they are. Some shut down. Others discount what they hear. Still others argue and even get angry. Why? Because most of us are raised with such warnings as "Don't let your head get too big!" or "Who do you think you are?" or "Aren't you just the conceited one!" We're not supposed to want to hear about our own virtues.

So when you are listening, pay attention to your resistances, those internal voices that reject and deny. Reveal your resistance maneuvers to your partner and ask him or her to help you focus on the love that wants to be expressed between you, instead of on the clichés that keep you hungry and unfulfilled. This will help deepen your intimacy and keep your romance alive and thriving.

3. As we've said, the First Passage opens you to the future and energizes the present. What you may have taken for granted in the past is now charged with vitality and spirit. Get into the habit of taking note of the little things you cherish: When he compliments you for a meal well prepared. The feel of her hand in yours. That he slows down when he's driving, in response to your having asked. How she respects you enough to ask, when you are reading, or at the computer, or watching television, if she can interrupt to tell you something.

Notice the little moments, what we call *small kindnesses,* and let each other know that those kindnesses are not being overlooked. Both of you will feel seen, heard, and appreciated. And your romance will thrive.

The Second Passage

The Clash of Differences
One Becomes Two

CHAPTER SEVEN

The Passion: The Initiation

$\mathcal{O}$ne minute you can't take your eyes off one another. The next minute all hell breaks loose. Your lover, who was brilliant, charming, mesmerizing, has suddenly become thick-headed, obnoxious, and belligerent. How did that happen? And why?

In the moment, it could be anything. A quirk. A habit. An attitude. That cute way he had of singing along with the car radio that made him seem so carefree and fun-loving, or the way she'd delicately dab at her lips with just the corner of her napkin, which looked so elegant and refined. But now his singing is insensitive and her manners are as applied as her lipstick and it's all making you crazy.

Your differences, which during the First Passage had the spell of love cast over them and seemed like gifts from God, are breaking through and dissolving the perfect oneness you thought was forever. Love is no longer blind and you begin to realize you are noticeably, undeniably, distinctly, and sometimes maddeningly different from one another!

You find yourselves arguing about who's right and who's wrong. What's the "correct" way to cut tomatoes. What's the "best" way to drive a car. You become embattled over politics or religion, anything that threatens your sense of security and the world you've constructed up to this point. The First Passage is definitely receding. You are graduating toward a more advanced level of love and intimacy and you cannot go back to the simple beginning.

Congratulations! You are entering *The Clash of Differences*, the Second Passage in the arc of love, the time when your separate and distinct identities must emerge.

Judith: When Jim and I were first together I hardly noticed what he wore. I was too caught up in his wonderful energy and sharp mind, his fun humor, and how honest and personal he was with me. I was in love in a way I'd never felt before.

But then, little by little, I started noticing things. For example, I noticed he wore what I thought were really dopey short-sleeved shirts. It wasn't so much the short-sleeved part I minded, it was the plaids and patterns that, as far as I was concerned, left a lot to be desired.

Where had he been keeping those shirts, I wondered? Why hadn't I seen them before? I knew I had to speak up. After all, I wanted to marry this man and I couldn't love him and harbor contempt at the same time.

Jim: When Judith told me she thought my choice of shirt patterns wasn't very elegant, as she put it, I became defensive. No one else had ever complained. And shirt patterns?! How petty!! Who did she think she was, the shirt-pattern maven of Western civilization??

At about the same time, it became clear that now and then, when Judith wanted something from me or wanted me to do something, like stop wearing those short-sleeved shirts, she'd ask me in baby talk. Here I thought

I was marrying an adult. I had to bring it to her attention and ask her to stop.

Judith: When he started pointing out my baby talk, he'd say "I'll
be glad to do what you want when you ask me as an adult.
You're not a child and I can't stand it when you approach
me like one." I was shocked!

For some of us, awareness of the differences surfaces in dribs
and drabs, a moment here, another there. For others, it takes
over in a swelling fit of disillusionment, fear, and pain, and the
relationship looks like it can't be salvaged and must end.

Please understand this is not necessarily a signal of failure.
You are being called to make a deeper connection with one
another and a deeper commitment to your relationship.

You might be tempted to give it all up because you never
imagined that love could ever hurt like this. But remember, love
has bigger designs on you than you have for yourself, and this
change in your relationship is *essential* for developing your capacity to love fully.

One Must Become Two

No matter how dazzling your love is at first, the time has come
when you must leave your madly-in-love oneness behind. The
feeling fades, and you stand before each other more and more
aware of your individuality.

That can feel like a distressing, even shocking distance. You
might say "I don't know you anymore," or wonder "What's become
of the person I fell in love with?" And the differences between
you, even the slightest gesture, can be an excruciating indication
of the gulf that seems impassable.

We worked with a couple, Moira and Evan, who were at their wits' end. They were bewildered by the sudden upsurge of discontentment they were both feeling. During our first session, when we asked them to describe what was most troubling, Moira turned to Evan and almost exploded.

"I can't believe your pinky sticks out when you hold a cup of coffee."

"What?" he blurted, completely unprepared for what she said.

"See?" she looked to us and then back to him, "You're not even aware you do it."

"You're right, I'm not. You never said a word to me. And instead you blindside me the first minute in counseling with that as your biggest complaint. What the hell is going on here?!"

"It isn't my biggest." She turned away and began to cry.

Once we settled them down, they told us that neither one had ever felt love for anyone like they felt for each other. That was part of why they were so confused and enraged. They were trapped by their own feelings. They didn't want their relationship to end, yet were afraid of each other and they both felt like they were walking on eggs. They hated seeing the other hurt and both felt responsible and guilty, but their trust had worn thin and the risk was too great to stay open.

"It used to be so magnificent," Evan whispered, lost and mystified. "Now being together is just grating, most of the time."

Though the bloom seemed to be off the rose, in fact the rose was just opening its petals to reveal more of itself, thorns and all. But why?

First, because the thorns are there. No one escapes them. We all bring what we are to our relationships and that means there will be clashes. Two different people cannot live in the intimacy of a long-term relationship and not crash into one another from time to time. You will either find that very threatening, or, as you more clearly understand the full arc of love and the purpose for each passage, you will know that Second Passage clashes are a gift to be worked through for the vitality, integrity, and ultimate comfort of your future together.

Second, as you learn to trust each other more and more, you will relax and what you've kept hidden, even from yourselves, will surface. That's part of what trust permits. While the clichéd idea of trust is that it makes everything effortless, that recognizes only the bright side. But there is also a dark side, and real trust opens those shadow doors as well. You can accept that as hopeful and healing, though sometimes unpleasant, only if you are willing to commit to making yourselves more fully available to the entirety of your relationship.

Most important, the thorns appear because part of your soul's responsibility is to test the quality of your love. If you cannot love your partner, thorns and all, then what you have, as sweet as it may be, cannot last.

Discovering that one or both of you cannot make it through the Second Passage, for whatever reason, is in itself a huge success—you then can go your separate ways and not make the mistake of marrying or having children.

When the need for identity separation becomes apparent and the struggle of reclaiming their individuality begins, people who naively believe that love should contain no pain, leap to the conclusion that their relationship is over. They don't know that love is the *cause* of a particular kind of heartache. Not the sentimental anguish of blazing passions that go unrequited, but the genuine distress of having to let go of the feeling of oneness, which is accompanied by the sense that something precious has been lost and will never be regained.

It wasn't long before Moira and Evan admitted they were both bitterly disillusioned. Nothing had prepared them for the painful and frightening struggle they found themselves in, and all they knew to do was blame each other.

As we walked them through the dynamics of the First Passage, they agreed with everything we said. When we described the process of the Second Passage, especially the heartache of disillusionment when people are unaware and unprepared, they relaxed, impressed with and comforted by the accuracy of what we were describing.

"You two have been through it, huh?" Moira asked.

"Yes, we have."

"That's good to know," Evan smiled.

It was clear they wanted to stay together and were willing to let us teach them what they needed to do to keep their relationship alive and growing.

The Second Passage in the arc of love is an initiation, a trial during which the two of you must learn to stand un-merged and distinct. It's the indispensable next step in the evolution of your relationship and the intimacy you are co-creating.

Without Differences There Is No Love

For your relationship to be real and supportive over time, and to keep romance alive, you both must feel you are loved for who you really are. Otherwise you can never be fully comfortable in the relationship and certainly never fully trusting. Without an awareness of and a respect for your differences, there can be no love.

Being Who You Really Are

For love to be meaningful, you have to feel free to express your thoughts and feelings with spontaneity and ease, confident that you are accepted "as is," in your delight as well as in your darkness. If you don't feel that acceptance, you live with the ongoing fear that sooner or later the "rest of you" will be exposed—in a fit of silliness, an untimely burst of anger, or a bout of depression. You'll never know what might trigger that terrible moment when you'll be found out and rejected, your deepest dread finally made real. To protect yourself against that horrible possibility, you tiptoe through your relationship trying to keep everything in control. That's no way to live and it kills love.

However, when you are accepted as is, that doesn't mean your partner won't want change and vice versa. The desire for change is as unavoidable as the fact of your differences. But whatever change either of you desires must always begin with who you are and build from there. Otherwise you will try to force yourself into being someone you're not.

If you try to satisfy your partner by trying to be somebody you're not, any change will be a pretense layered upon an underlying pretense, which is like building a house on quicksand. You will have failed not at love, but at not creating any love at all. Love loves what is real. That is the only foundation that will allow you to trust your life together.

There Must Be a Between

For love to be, there must be a between. In other words, there must be two individuals, each with their own identity, aware and protective of the psychological and spiritual space between them. It's in that space that their relationship is co-created. It's in that space that romance and intimacy can be kept alive.

While this may sound obvious, it isn't. For example, how many relationships have you known in which one person dominated the other? How many couples have you met who are in a perpetual power struggle, one winning in one moment, the other in the next? How many marriages have you seen in which two people had nothing to say to each other? In each of these instances, there is no between.

In the first, one person submits, which is the same as becoming invisible. There is no between, just one person with all the power.

In the second, two people jockey for power. One is in charge, then the other takes over, both lost in a fruitless struggle.

In the last, both people vanished long ago. They don't even see each other anymore.

Love and intimacy take two equal people, each showing up to be counted, standing present so that they can bring their relationship to life across the full arc of love. When they make themselves present, love has the opportunity to live between them. Then the two strangers who became as one in the First Passage, now become two.

Commitment Must Be to the Relationship

Many men and women believe that to be in a loving relationship they must wholly commit to the *other person*. We hear it in phrases like "I'm his" or "I am devoted to her." But no matter how romantic it may sound to say "I'm his" or "I'm hers," if you actually give yourself to another person, even if it is the person you feel so much love for, you're setting yourself up to become invisible.

What if there are aspects of your lover that you don't like? Or that disappoint you? Or even frighten you? Are you committed to those? If not, then are you truly committed to the other person? Or are you only partially truly committed? That doesn't even make sense, does it?

However, you *can* commit, heart and soul, to your relationship—to that which exists between you. When you do, you can express the strength of your desire to be with your lover by fully showing up for the life you are co-creating. Your relationship becomes the vessel into which you invest your emotional, intellectual, sexual, and spiritual gifts and needs, and through which you experience the affection and intimacy that is at the heart of love.

Only recently, and only in those cultures that support individuality, has the idea made sense that two separate and equally empowered persons could co-create a relationship centered in love, romance, and intimacy. Historically, the couple was subservient to the needs of the community. Whether they loved or even liked each other was unimportant, and romance was feared as too disruptive.

Now, however, with most cultures in the world accepting the idea of the *individual,* two people can actually co-create ways for each of them to retain their sense of self while at the same time being a couple. You don't have to lose yourself to be loved. In fact, it is only when you maintain a solid sense of yourself that love and real romance are possible.

Rooted in Your Wholeness

The First Passage opens what is possible and is a foretelling of what your relationship can evolve into, but it is not yet rooted in the complexity of who the two of you are in your fullness. The merger at the beginning of love feels safe and secure, because your darker and more perplexing differences haven't yet shown up. When they do, you will feel thrown into uncertainty as the necessary separation, provoked by your differences, begins.

It is critical to understand that when two people have not been prepared for their clash of differences, they can feel as though they've been betrayed. In fact, that experience is quite common. It can lead them to express their insecurity in hateful and hurtful ways—name-calling, character assaults, ultimatums that demand instant change. Both men and women can become abusive, blaming each other as they vent the rage they feel at the disillusionment and the loss of "perfect" closeness.

But while the Second Passage can sometimes evoke drastic behaviors, it also abhors pretense and performance. It will not tolerate overly practiced "ladylike" and "gentlemanly" posing that masks what you consider unspeakable. Love strives to make the unspeakable speakable, otherwise you are stuffed with thoughts and feelings you cannot reveal and nothing can relieve the pressure. So *The Clash of Differences* works to burn away what is false, anything that prevents both people from being forthcoming with who they are.

We understand that you may be afraid to feel emotionally separate from your precious lover, the person who, it seems like just moments ago, was entwined around and within you. But for your love to grow it is absolutely necessary for the First Passage to fade and for you to consciously work to reclaim your own individuality.

The Fear of Differences

We know from the work we've done with thousands and thousands of people, across the country and internationally, that almost everyone has been raised to feel threatened by people who are different. That fear of differences, which is for the most part unconscious, prevents us from being truly available for an intensely satisfying, spiritually meaningful love.

So we ask you this question: What were you taught, either overtly or covertly, by your parents, extended family, those in your neighborhood or church, about those who were different from your group? What were you taught to think of them and how were you taught to treat them?

Here's a sampling of answers we routinely receive from the people at our workshops:

- You can't trust anyone but your family.

- You can date them, but never marry one.

- They're beneath you.

- They think they're something special.

- Their politics are dangerous.

- They're from the wrong religion.

- People like that never amount to anything.

- Spoiled rotten, all of them.

No matter our backgrounds, we all learn something about the danger of opening to, being curious about, or trusting those who are different.

Here's another question: How were you treated for the ways you were different from everyone else in your immediate family?

Typical answers we hear from workshop attendees are that they were told:

- You're too loud.

- You think you know it all.

- You've always got your nose in a book.

- You're not fooling anybody!

- You think you're better than everyone else.

- Why must you be so dramatic?

- We don't do that in this house, do you hear me?

Whether the lessons are hidden or blatantly obvious, the upshot is that anyone who is different is seen as a threat. No matter how enlightened we believe we are, we carry an unconscious internal anxiety, an unconscious readiness to reject anyone who is different, including ourselves.

So what's the big deal? Isn't it wise to be wary of strangers?

Perhaps. But consider this. You are also expected to grow up, date, marry, and live happily ever after. However, your spouse cannot help but be different from you as you are different from him or her.

As long as you are unaware of your unconscious beliefs about being different, you may try to control your anxiety by seeking to make the other person into what you believe they *should* be. Or you may try to conform to what you perceive he or she thinks is the right way for you to be.

In either case, your marriage will be built on a very unstable foundation: the fear of one another's differences, and the need to control your thoughts and feelings and those of your partner, to keep that fear at bay. That is a recipe for disaster, not love. And it's sure to keep you afraid.

When you enter the Second Passage, your differences rush in to stir the pot. You can feel as though the very nature of love is being undermined. But that's not the case. It is your *fear* of those differences that must be exposed, or you will never have the kind of intimacy, trust, and romance that will make a long-term relationship meaningful and fulfilling.

Love Needs the Differences

No matter how you imagine human life was created, it is an amazing fact that you exist. Whatever you think it was that made it possible for you to be here—the Big Bang, the Lawfulness of the Universe, God creating everything from nothing, or God expressing creation through the Big Bang—the fact is you are here, in all your distinct individuality.

Love needs you to be different from one another. For that very reason your lover must show up as someone who is not you, regardless of what you have in common, so that he or she will be able to recognize your uniqueness even when you cannot. Of course, you do the same in return.

But if you are alike, then what does being an individual mean? If you are alike, what does intimacy mean? If you are alike, what is love for?

Think of it this way. In some moment, when your lover feels more love for you than you do for yourself, you are being invited to experience the love you cannot give to yourself. Unless your partner is separate and distinct from you, such a love will not be available. It is in the differences between you that the possibility exists for you to have a love unlike anything you've ever known before.

That is just one reason why love *requires* differences.

So it's important that you both acknowledge your entrance into the Second Passage and honor the realities that are visiting you. Your soul is calling you to become even more present, even more real. You must find out whether your commitment is secure enough, your bond deep enough, your willingness open-ended enough to form a solid foundation upon which you will build your lives, individually and together. It is your lives you are investing, so this is no small issue.

Most people betray love by fleeing at the first sign of conflict. But if your relationship is to thrive, you must appreciate that conflict is a stepping stone to emotional and spiritual growth. The obstacles are teachers in the course of your growing maturity.

Reassure each other that *The Clash of Differences* is a natural part of the full arc of love and that you are still committed to being together. Recognize that you are becoming allies, even though it may not feel that way at times. The Second Passage is a time of exploring and integrating the necessity for each of you to be your own person. It is the process of becoming two differentiated people, each with a sense of self that is clear and distinct.

Exploring
The Clash of Differences

1. The Second Passage leads you into the darker aspects of what it takes to co-create a solid relationship. Rather than withdraw from this truth, admit it. Make a point of telling each other how conflict was handled in your household. You cannot help but have picked up some of those traits. However, now you are in different circumstances, so watch out for how you experience and express conflict in the way your family did.

2. Announce to yourselves with some kind of special celebration that this new, quite troublesome passage has arrived. Perhaps you'll prepare a primitive feast to honor the upsetting realities that are visiting you. Or you'll create a memorial service for the effortlessness that is receding in order to make room for new life between you. Or maybe you'll go camping, hiking—anything that reminds you that much of life's value involves earthy, sometimes gritty stuff.

3. To honor your differences, alternate taking each other out for adventures that introduce your partner to aspects of yourself you want him or her to be aware of and learn about.

For example, take her to play pool, take him to your favorite dance club, take her to that special spot in the woods where you sit and watch the birds, take him junk shopping, take her to the movie you've already seen three times, take him snowshoeing. Describe to your partner what you love about each activity and why you want to be known in this particular way.

When you are the invitee, even if you don't personally enjoy the activity, open yourself to the intimate gift of new awareness about your beloved.

CHAPTER EIGHT

The Purpose:
Separate and Distinct

*O*kay, so you're at each other, irritated, annoyed. Tempers flare. Little things explode out of proportion. And we've said "Congratulations! Welcome to *The Clash of Differences.*"

"Come on! Are you two crazy?" Is that what you're saying to yourself? Or are you thinking that we're in never-never land, seeing only what is right about everything? Well, we're not crazy, but the "seeing what's right" part holds true for us, though it's not always easy.

When *A Glimpse of What Is Possible* gives way to *The Clash of Differences,* your soul is telling you that, if you want to grow as a couple, you can no longer stay in the romance of the Garden of Eden. You must move on to face your emotional and psychological nakedness together. You may put on what amount to defensive fig leaves and plead for a return to the enchantment, but your pleas will go unanswered, because the primary spiritual purpose of the Second Passage is to press you to expand the love you share.

The beginning was free. Now you must grow and mature further, clearing the way for the greater love that wants to live between you.

Rude Awakenings

We all know the story of Adam and Eve. They sinned, and as their punishment they were cast out of Eden. Well, perhaps there's another interpretation. Perhaps their time in Eden was their emotional and spiritual infancy. If they had stayed, they would have remained like children, capable only of obedience. To have a full and transcendent love, for one another and for their God, they had to learn about differences. She and he. Only then could they recognize the way the Creator created them—*man and woman created He them*. They had to learn to *choose* love rather than wait for love to choose them.

Perhaps God thought, "It is now time for *you*, not I, to determine how you are going to know each other and live your lives. If you choose wisely, the Garden shall be yours again, but only through your own effort and success in learning how to live as equals inside the love you create and are created by."

Even under this interpretation, leaving Eden would have come as a shock, a rude awakening, because they would have had to look to their own resources instead of expecting to be provided for.

When you were born and the doctor slapped you on the butt to awaken you to this life, that was a rude transition from the womb world where your mother's body supplied everything for you, including oxygen. But the doctor had to shock your lungs into working so you could breathe on your own, otherwise you would not have survived.

The onset of the Second Passage can feel as rude and uncomfortable as being cast out of Paradise or being squeezed through the birth canal and promptly swatted. Suddenly, stunningly, things are not what they were.

Sometimes your partner seems unrecognizable and you wonder how you ever got involved. Sometimes you feel oddly different, not like the you you've always known. But if your relationship is going to breathe on its own, things must change.

Love is a paradox. On the one hand, it is fiercely possessive. It claims you for its own, demanding that you give yourself over and let it lead. If you don't surrender, you're sure to stay stuck in a pattern of unsatisfying feelings and failed expectations and then blame love for not showing you an intimacy that actually works.

But on the other hand, you cannot be passive when love stirs. Love insists that you consciously create the vessel in which it will be received, because love will not enter where it is not truly taken in.

From one side you must surrender and listen, and from the other side you must assert yourself and choose to take action. A paradox indeed. But that is the nature of love.

The ambition of the Second Passage is to coax you, push you, tear you, drag you if necessary, away from outmoded, limited, rigid ways of thinking about love, relationship, and even yourself. Your world will sometimes feel like it's been turned upside down. In fact, if you don't feel that way sometimes, you're only doing what you've already done and you'll end up right back where you've already been.

At this point, love is a trial by fire, the fire of consciousness, seeking to burn off what is not authentic and will stand in the way of your co-creating the fullness of being together.

Lois and Kim

When they met, Kim devoured Lois with his eyes. He thought she was one of the "hottest babes" he'd ever seen. As their relationship got hotter, he cooked for her and then fed her in bed after making love. She loved to dance and do a striptease for him. They were inseparable and married in three months.

Very soon after they married, Lois began to make demands on Kim that he found threatening, both financially and emotionally. She couldn't feel he loved her "unless she was well taken care of"—and she meant that from the bottom of her poverty-ridden childhood. Since he was a CPA and earned good money, Lois insisted that the money she made as a dental hygienist remain hers and that Kim should support them both.

Kim was terrified of confronting her with how unreasonable and unfair she was being. He didn't want to lose her and all he knew to do was revert to being the obedient boy who had worked so hard to please his emotionally insatiable mother.

Little by little, Kim's resentment mounted and he started staying later at work. Lois was furious. She would get back at him by withholding sex. *The Clash of Differences* was moving into prime time. They never did talk with one another about what was really bothering them and they were left with the unfortunate stereotypes of the moneygrubbing woman and the emotionally shutdown man, rather than discovering the underlying causes of their distress.

Sometimes It Doesn't Work Out

It can happen that the fire of consciousness will burn up the relationship if it is rooted more in fantasy than in reality. For example, the thrill of being with a wealthy man will subside when he pays more attention to his golf pro than to you, or when he insists that you play hostess at his business events whether you like it or not, or when he tells you to "keep your petty personal problems to yourself."

Or, you meet an ambitious and enterprising woman who runs her mother's Chinese takeout business, and you're intrigued until you find that she will only date you on Saturday nights because she's always exhausted. When you ask to be with her more often, she tells you you're annoying her with your neediness.

Anything similar to these examples will certainly come as an awakening of the rude kind.

If you are wise, you'll use your shock as a wake-up call informing you that your priorities are out of sync with what your soul wants. You will need to dig deeper into yourself to discover what led you to be so enthralled by someone who was not available for a loving relationship with you. Hint: How was the person similar to an unavailable parent? Your discovery can turn your painful experience into a life-altering success!

Being Psychologically and Spiritually Visible

Emotional separation is necessary for psychological and spiritual visibility. If the oneness of the First Passage did not recede, and make room for both of you to acknowledge one another as different, then intimacy would not be possible. Intimacy takes two, each of you separate and distinct in your own right, each of you willing to be revealed and eager to learn about the other as well as yourselves—as two equal individuals in relationship.

Judith: When we were in the process of writing this book, Jim came into my office and asked for clarification of a phrase I'd written. I was the lead writer and Jim did the first rewrite and edits. Sometimes it's the other way around, depending upon what we're writing.

Jim: Judith had used the phrase "fiercely possessive," and in context I didn't understand what she meant.

Judith: I explained what I was doing, but Jim thought the word "insistent" was more appropriate. We went back and forth and we weren't getting anywhere except more and more frustrated.

We were each caught up in our own point of view, trying to convince the other of the rightness of our positions. Rather than standing confident in our own separate identities and able to hear one another, we were isolated, defensive, and stuck, and in a very real sense, invisible to each other. The words, "possessive" and "insistent," were not merely a problem of semantics, but they also represented our subtle yet very different experiences of what each word meant.

Jim: It takes two unique selves to be separate, but only one self-centered point of view to be isolated. When we realized that what we were talking about was our two distinct experiences, rather than the meaning of words, I was able to acknowledge Judith's experience of "fiercely possessive," as she was my experience of "insistent." In that sense, we remained distinct and we were able to learn about each other and from each other. Then we were connected in our mutual appreciation of the other's individuality. But that was only possible when we became visible as two different people with two different experiences, neither one right or wrong. Just different.

We cannot stress this enough. A relationship cannot succeed unless there are two distinct persons recognizing each other across the ways they are different. Otherwise there are only two isolates pretending to feel connected.

When we were quarreling, we were detached—from one another and from our knowledge that quarrels can only happen when our emotional connection is broken. There was distortion on both sides. We had reduced one another to objects, adversaries to be manipulated and overcome, rather than seeing the real people we loved and cared about, each with legitimate points of view. When we lost the connection, we fell into our own isolated, self-righteous worlds, capable of imagining all kinds of threats and hurts and "necessary" defenses that can only be born of fear.

When we finally came to our senses, we stopped being defensive and started listening to each other. Our feelings returned, for ourselves and one another, and the connection was present again. But please keep in mind that our connection was only possible when we could experience each other as psychologically and spiritually separate, unique and distinct, and then open our curiosity to one another. In the intimacy that followed, we were able to arrive at a resolution of the "word problem" that satisfied both of us.

Love *is* fiercely possessive, sweeping you away and claiming you for its own. And love *does* insist that you willfully participate in the process of receiving it. We saw that love is *both* possessive and insistent, and we did so *because* we were different.

Love is not a straight-line process. What happened between us with our "word problem" is a small example of how Second Passage–type issues can arise even when two people have, for the most part, passed through the trials of reclaiming their own distinctiveness. That's why it is critical for you to integrate an awareness of what Second Passage struggles feel like, so that, as your relationship evolves, you will be equipped with the skills to notice and resolve such issues as they arise.

Resilience and Commitment

The Second Passage is necessarily a very unsettling time. Unconscious material—what's called "emotional baggage"—that has been lying dormant is awakened and exposed by the jolt of love's intensity. You are dislodged from your emotional comfort zones, and from the safe harbor that is part of the First Passage, and it can feel as though you've been thrust back into issues you thought departed with acne and braces.

Baggage is usually experienced as old doubts about your worth and lovability, fears about being hurt and abandoned, or, on the flip side, narcissistic rage about not being appreciated and valued the way you think you deserve.

The Second Passage is a mandatory tour of your unconscious personal baggage. Its purpose is to test your resilience and commitment. Sometimes you will feel so emotionally contorted that you're sure you look like a pretzel. But can you spring back and continue? Will you trust your relationship enough to go through the trials that will test your emotional and spiritual promise to make it work?

You both bring baggage. If you will not or cannot acknowledge that, you will eventually shortchange your relationship. Either it will end, sending you in your own directions, or it will continue lifelessly, imprisoning you in an orbit of rage and recrimination. But either way, you will have abandoned love—not the other way around.

Don't fear the differences between you. Embrace them. Sometimes they will cause friction and even conflict. But when you hold the well-being of your relationship as your first priority, you understand that you need each other and you will need the ways you are different to co-create what you have. Then your relationship will truly reflect who both of you actually are. In that sense there will be separation, an acknowledgment that the one you love is an *other*, full and equal in his or her own integrity, a thrill to love and be loved by.

Conflict

The world's foremost spiritual teachers have taught that to expand consciousness you have to go through some kind of personal transformation—what we're calling a *passage.*

Awakened vision is possible only after you have faced into a demanding challenge—in the Second Passage it is usually in the form of conflict—and let go of whatever limiting beliefs stand in your way. A new and different awareness awaits you on the other side of your trial, a larger and more encompassing consciousness.

An intimate relationship, no matter how wonderful, is the perfect vehicle for those challenges. Conflict is unavoidable. Two unique people might quarrel with one another about disciplining the children, handling the in-laws, spending money. They might even fight when one feels neglected or the other feels invaded.

Please don't make the mistake of assuming that conflict is only negative.

As we said in our first book, *The New Intimacy,* a conflict is like an SOS emerging from the recesses of your relationship. Understand that its purpose is to alert you that something needs attention. Something in your relationship is calling out for change, a change that will be inspired by love and will make room for more love.

When you embrace the challenge of differences—which is at the core of spiritual awakening—you have the opportunity to grow each time you and your partner find yourselves in conflict. Spiritual change is a metamorphosis, like carbon becoming diamond. That change cannot take place without a spiritual workout. And sometimes it takes a serious struggle with a well-intentioned partner to inspire your transformation.

But What If . . . ?

But what if she's wrong, plain and simple? But what if he doesn't know what he's talking about?

What if two people are in a conflict over something factual? Who was the third president of the United States? How far is the earth from the sun? The answer is indisputable. Even if it's a conflict over something that is factual within a range—for instance, the optimum blood pressure is 120 over 80, but it depends upon age, body type, and other factors—there is nonetheless a factual answer. All the couple needs to do is refer to some source for confirmation. One of them will be right and the other wrong and that should settle the matter. If they continue arguing or even fighting, then the fight is not about facts but about something personal that is hidden within the storm.

Conflicts between intimates are almost never about facts but about feelings. One or both of them has been hurt in some way, either in terms of how they are actually treating each other—ignoring, taking for granted, dismissing, bullying, not listening—or in their interpretations of what is taking place. And those interpretations are laden with the baggage they brought with them from before they ever met. These conflicts have no ready references, no easy, indisputable answers. Resentments and disappointments are never objective, especially for those who claim to be reasonable and want to "keep it logical."

Conflicts always take place in those areas of your relationship where you haven't worked things out. We call that your *emotional wilderness*. You are out at the edges, where the emotional terrain is rocky and hidden potholes can be anywhere. There is no clear map, so it's easy to misunderstand and misinterpret what's happening. And neither of you has *the* way. If you are going to reach a resolution that is mutually beneficial, you must accept that both of you have a piece of the truth and both of you are distorting the issue due to your emotional baggage. If there were no distortions there would be no conflicts. You must uncover the distortions and integrate both points of view, otherwise one of you will be left out and that will create bitterness and futility, which will only fester and lead to more conflict.

Conflict Styles

The Second Passage is a time of testing. It is also a time to learn about your conflict styles. Most of us learned in our family of origin to approach or avoid conflict in ways that are seriously detrimental to love. Therefore the more you know about your conflict style(s), the better prepared you will be for growing further in love.

Which of these conflict styles best describe you?

Conflict-avoidant: You'll do anything to avoid disagreements or confrontations, including going against your own desire, your own well-being. Your motto is "Peace at any price."

Passive-aggressive: You won't speak up about what is troubling you, you'll just thwart your partner's happiness in very indirect ways. Your motto is "Don't get angry, get even."

Self-abusive: You take everything personally and assume that all difficulties are either caused by you or have to be solved by you. Your motto is "I'm sorry, it's all my fault."

Other-abusive: You blame your partner for everything. Absolutely everything. So you always feel innocent. Your motto is "I must defend myself at all costs."

Power-struggler: You're certain you are right and your partner is wrong. Unfortunately, your partner is certain you are wrong and he or she is right. The challenge is in trying to persuade your partner of his or her wrongness. Your motto is "I have to win, no matter what."

Paranoid: You are suspicious that your lover is trying to hurt you, manipulate you, drive you crazy. You're always leery and distrustful of the one you claim to love. Your motto is "I can never know what my partner is up to."

Narcissistic: You are shocked whenever your lover disagrees with you because it is inconceivable that there is any other position than your own. Your motto is "You think what?!"

Silent but deadly: You feel hurt and stop speaking, sometimes for days on end. Your motto is "I'll make 'em pay."

Helpless: You throw up your hands in futility, and start to cry and whine about how hopeless it all is. Your motto is "I can never get this right."

Frozen: Your brain turns to ice, your tongue is stuck in your mouth, and you feel rigid throughout your whole body. Your motto is "I'm screwed no matter what I do."

None of these types is pure. You may have a mix-and-match approach to conflict. The point is to use your clash of differences to recognize and communicate how you handle conflict. That will open you to be more available to your relationship. And it will bond you more deeply as you reveal more and more of who you are.

As you remain aware of the important purposes of the Second Passage, you will mine the treasures of this difficult but essential time and you will mature toward a deeper relationship and a sweeter intimacy than you can even imagine.

Exploring
The Clash of Differences

1. The arc of love is a process that is inspired and guided by the soul.

    So before you fall asleep at night, ask your soul—perhaps you call it your higher consciousness or your inner wisdom—what needs to fall away in the Second Passage. What are you clinging to that is so precious you would rather be loyal to it than to the commitment you've made to your partner and yourself? Perhaps it's your fear of being hurt, your unwillingness to go against parental teachings, or an image of yourself as unworthy of being loved.

    In your journal write the responses you hear or think or feel. These messages may not make "sense" at first, but don't let that get in the way. And the next morning be sure to read what you've written. The messages from your own conscious and unconscious mind will become clear over time.

2. You must avoid blaming each other and you must reaffirm that what you are going through is necessary. When you cast blame, you are divesting yourself of responsibility, making your partner responsible for everything that's going wrong. But in any conflict between two intimates, both people are always contributing to their difficulties. That is a fact. You are responsible to some degree. For the sake of your relationship,

stop using blame as a crutch and start looking at what you are both doing that leads to your conflicts.

Promise to catch each other whenever either of you is using blame. That will open you to what needs to be let go, to be burned away so you can evolve into deeper and deeper intimacy and romance.

3. The Second Passage is not a struggle in every moment. You will feel constant tension only if you never express your feelings and needs and never make yourself emotionally available. That's emotional constipation.

When you are both feeling at ease, share with each other how you see your own conflict style(s) and how you see the way(s) your lover handles conflict. Again, you cannot blame one another nor argue or contradict one another. You must listen with respect. That will prevent you from falling into the trap of taking this personally and it will help you more clearly see what each of you does when things get hot. Self-knowledge is always a buffer against things spinning out of control.

CHAPTER NINE

The Problems:
This Can't Be Love

How often have you been out to dinner with another couple and the conversation went something like this . . .

She: We had such a marvelous fight last night! It took us to new depths of understanding ourselves and one another.

He: Oh, sure we had to yell and shout a little at first. We were both so frustrated and angry about how things had been.

She: But after we settled down and really started listening to each other's complaints, and you know that isn't always easy, we could see that each of us needed to make some changes to better express the love we feel and to create a new facet of our relationship.

He: It was so exciting to see one another in this new light and to know we can keep growing and learning like this for the rest of our lives together.

How often? We'll bet the answer is rarely or never.

But that's only because the notion that conflict can be healthy, a catalyst for emotional and spiritual growth, is a new concept in the realm of real romance. So it's likely to be considered pure hogwash. Well, it is pure hogwash if you are devoted to ideas such as love never breeds anger or happy lovers never quarrel. The truth is, love *can* breed anger and happy lovers *do* quarrel, and anyone who's been in a real relationship knows that.

It's about How You Think

The most difficult and most painful problems of the Second Passage, particularly at the outset, are the result of how you think about what is happening.

Conflict is inevitable. Why? Because you are different from one another. You cannot live in the intimacy of your life together without crashing into each other from time to time. In fact, conflict is a necessary part of the way you will deepen your understanding of who you are, individually and together. With that in mind, it's just a matter of learning how to handle your conflicts so that you maximize the results for both of you.

But, as you know, clarity of mind easily slips away when your feelings are hurt. So here are several significant mistakes couples can make during the Second Passage.

This Can't Be Love

When you are unprepared for the Second Passage, you can be shocked, even shattered by unexpected eruptions from the underbelly of commitment and intimacy. You might believe that if a relationship is "meant to be," the romantic high will last forever.

Then when conflict appears you tell yourself, "This can't be love. Love is supposed to be only wonderful." You decide your relationship is a disaster and you break it off. That's a very simplistic and fantasy-driven way to think about love and romance. It leaves no room for the real people you are and your real, complex, and sometimes upsetting ways of being.

You might not be very cheery in the mornings. Or you might not deal with sickness very well. Or you might be afraid of not having enough money, or you might not care about money at all. You bring your personal disposition to your relationship, and not all that you are will match or be immediately compatible with your partner. There are bound to be times when who you are will clash with who your partner is. That's unavoidable, so you can expect conflict—from mild to serious.

For "only wonderful" to exist, you would have to manipulate yourself into being agreeable, charming, and affectionate at all times. If you did that, *you* would be lost. You would be a fake, and the real you would, no surprise, be feeling depressed beneath all that smiling and forced behavior. None of us nor our relationships can withstand that kind of emptiness layered over with pretense.

Struggle does not mean that there is something wrong with your relationship. Conflict is simply a call for change. Knowing that will spur you to grow and find deeper, more fulfilling connection.

Please note that even though the Second Passage entails conflict, verbal or physical abuse is absolutely and totally unacceptable and without justification. By abuse we mean the serious, willful intention to do psychological or physical harm. If you believe you are the recipient of abuse, you must insist that it stop. Immediately. If your partner refuses to respect your demand, then you must leave.

Also, do not use false accusations of abuse to get the upper hand. That's just exploiting your partner's vulnerabilities to your own advantage and that *definitely* is abuse.

Furthermore, the abuse you are feeling may just be your feeling. If you were abused in childhood it would be easy for you to feel upset over a raised voice, even helpful criticism or a heated argument. Many behaviors can make you *feel* abused. Don't confuse what is going on now with what happened in your past.

To help prevent that confusion, explain your past abuse to your lover so he or she can be aware of your susceptibility to misinterpreting what's happening now. Then enlist your partner as an ally to help you stay grounded in your present-time reality.

Personal Suffering

When you lack an understanding of what Second Passage love requires, it's easy to feel sorry for yourself and conclude that "this shouldn't be happening to me," or "I must not be very lovable," or "I've given so much, why can't I find a love that works?" The Second Passage is often tough. We respect that. But if you begin to feel sorry for yourself and victimized by your relationship, you will be adding a layer of self-inflicted suffering to the actual pain of what you're going through.

Suffering, as distinct from pain, is a result of the way you think about what is happening. An expression of pain might be "This sure is tough. I wonder what we have to do to get through it." It is direct and focused on the events at hand. An expression of suffering might be "Other couples never had to go through this," which is a shift into fantasy that serves only to add further burden to your experience and your relationship.

An example of a deeper pain might be expressed as "I never knew I had this much loneliness inside me," which is a moment of self-discovery that can promote healing. Suffering, in this case, might be "I must not be meant for love." That is a flight into self-pity.

When you permit suffering, you become victimized by your own insistence on how things should be and your rejection of how things are.

Emotional Cheating

The disruption and distress of the Second Passage is seldom limited to the two people involved. Disappointment and hurt feelings drive the chaos that spills over into phone conversations and lunchroom commiserations as frustrated lovers tell their heart-wrenching tales. They are desperate for advice, but most of what they get is given from the same divisive and blaming perspective that created the problems in the first place.

Instead of the couple facing into their conflicts together, sorting out their responsibilities, looking for resolutions, using their time to learn more about themselves and one another, one or both of them turns to others for emotional satisfaction—be they friends, relatives, co-workers, a minister, priest, rabbi, or even a therapist. These outsiders are expected to analyze and dissect "the girlfriend's behavior" or "the husband's strange reactions." Mothers are required to take sides. Psychics are called upon to solve the problem. Anyone who might offer even the slightest hope of providing help suddenly becomes a confidante and is given the most private details.

But taking your problems outside your relationship is emotional cheating.

We're not saying that when you're in a conflict you shouldn't go to someone you trust to sort out your thoughts and feelings. That can be very helpful. But if you don't return to your partner and deal with your difficulties together, you are cheating emotionally on your relationship.

Emotional cheating is far more pervasive than sexual cheating because it's not considered cheating. And, like sexual cheating, it is often very melodramatic—and certainly destructive—because it is a substitute for what is actually needed.

If you are in the habit of going to others for advice and sympathy, please change your priorities and make staying within the emotional bounds of your relationship your primary concern. Only then will the Second Passage bring you its enormous payoff. Either there will be a clear refusal to do the lovework by one or both of you, in which case it will be time to part, or you will enjoy deepened intimacy, proven trust, and the confidence to go forward. Either way, you cannot fail.

Feeling Hopeless

When you're feeling not-good-enough, it's easy to fall into hopelessness as *The Clash of Differences* collides with your self-doubt. You want so badly for your relationship to work out, and now, it seems, no matter what you do, it's all so messy, so upsetting. Nothing like you imagined.

Hopelessness arises when you take your focus from the issues immediately at hand and, consciously or unconsciously, begin imagining the worst of all outcomes. You leave the present, project yourself into a desolate future, and are paralyzed by what you see. Giving up seems reasonable and you fall into a pit of self-imposed heartache and suffering.

Furthermore, if you're not aware of the passages in the full arc of love, then hopelessness is not only expected but it's almost inevitable. You won't have the awareness to prevent imaginings from overwhelming you.

When you face into the demands of the Second Passage and learn from them, then even if your relationship doesn't work out, you should not think of it as a failure. It will be a success because you will have been opened to more of the truth of who you are and what you want, and you will be that much more prepared for the next relationship.

Lack of Spiritual Awareness

Perhaps you see no other purpose for a romantic relationship than companionship and sex, fun and family. If so, you'll be very disillusioned and feel betrayed when the Second Passage arrives. You won't have the emotional foundation to see it as a spur for your growth and that of your partner, your love, and your relationship. When you see the demands of the Second Passage as a training ground for deep intimacy, you are open to learning to integrate the inevitable changes so your relationship stays always fresh and new.

You now know there is a larger purpose for your being together—your evolving individual and shared wholeness. And since you feel equipped to recognize, at any time, where along the arc you are, you become progressively aware of the expansive and unfolding future of your relationship. You become more and more of a couple. Neither of you has to lose your independence, and you can appreciate the blessings of your oneness while remaining separate and distinct.

What You're Used To

For some of you, anger and what can only be described as dirty fighting are commonplace. That was pretty much all you saw your parents do. They yelled and screamed and raised their fists. So being hit and called names by people who were supposed to love you just came with being alive.

You grew up with a misguided association between love and rage, passion and abuse. Now, if you're not being pushed around physically and/or emotionally, you can't feel loved. You have no basis for sexual excitement, so you'll work to provoke trouble any-time you're feeling bored or unloved or unalive.

For those of you who think this is overstated and part of the "therapeutic culture," think again. Such distorted associations are widespread, and those who are burdened with them live with a continual confusion between what they hear love is supposed to be like and what they actually experience. Yet, when a thera-pist tries to point out the source of their heartache, they will fiercely defend the family they came from. They need to keep everything hidden because they live with a haunting fear that if they faced the truth it would release a despair that seems like it would never end.

Staying in allegiance with your family's ways keeps you unavail-able for anything but your parents' world, a world in which you cannot be anything but their child, no matter your age.

It's about What You Do

The Clash of Differences is so threatening for so many people that they become desperate, acting out in ways that are either distracting or devastating to the love that could be.

Playing Rhett and Scarlett

Gone with the Wind is one of the most revered love stories in American culture. It's an example of the excitement generated by chronically playing the game of seduce-and-conquer.

When Rhett surrenders, Scarlett can only slap his face. When Scarlett melts, Rhett's off to a poker game. They never give them-selves to their relationship at the same time.

But what tension! What excitement! What suspense!

That's what a lot of couples do to distract themselves from the larger challenge of their differences. They throw fits of rage and break up—and not, as you might imagine, so they can then make up. Every breakup is painful, maybe even ugly. Then they get back together and the heavenly romance of the beginning takes over. At first.

But their reconciliation is only a facade and soon they're again fighting, blaming each other, weeping, storming out. If they're married, they file for divorce but don't proceed with it. The fact is they never deal with what is causing their distress, because as long as they are playing by the loveless rules of seduce-and-conquer, distress is certain. They're caught in a merry-go-rebound of their own making. How dramatic. How intense. How futile!

Let's Get Married and Have a Baby

Rather than accepting the Second Passage as a necessary step in the arc of love, many men and women try to flee by doing something drastic. He'll say, "All right. If you want to know where you stand, let's get married. At least that'll prove I love you." They do and it's no proof at all.

She decides, without telling him, that she'll stop taking the pill, thinking, "He'll have to shape up when the baby comes along and he has a family to support." Then the pressures of a new baby turn them both into infants who cannot stop quarreling. The baby is left to be raised by parents who are little more than children themselves.

Rather than learning how to relate in a mature, productive manner, they burden their already overstrained commitment and accentuate what is not working.

Plunging headlong into binding commitments like marriage or parenthood as a way to solve existing problems is simply evidence that the people involved are too immature for the responsibilities they're signing up for.

Abuse It or Lose It

With some men and women, their sense of self is so fragile and so undeveloped, they desperately need people to be just like them in order to feel secure. During the First Passage their lover is everything they've ever dreamed of and the sense of sameness they feel is unbelievable.

But then, when their beloved starts revealing attitudes and feelings that are different, up comes their insecurity and they feel desperate. They are overwhelmed by fear and they strike out abusively. Whether it's in words or by actions, they need their fury as fuel to protect themselves from the threat of their lover being different. It's the only power they have, the only way they can imagine forcing their lover back into meeting their rigid expectations.

If differences were permitted, their fragile self stands to be exposed, an option that to them is unthinkable. They literally cannot imagine that love could spring from being different, that life could be richer, fuller through sharing differences. So, from their desperate, isolated, and loveless point of view, either they choose abusive control or they believe that all is lost.

I'd Rather Dream about It

Many people are addicted to a facsimile of love. They create perfect fantasies in which everyone, especially their "lover," behaves in just the ways they want them to. It's a dreamland in which all is good—feels good, looks good, sounds good, smells good, and even tastes good! But ultimately it isn't very good, because it isn't real.

Too many people prefer avoiding what it takes to live love in reality. Romance novels, pornography, and even simple daydreams can be hugely arousing, but they never lead to the Second Passage. Trouble-free, hot, and stimulating auto-erotic "love." What could be better? Well, nothing if what you really want is to be alone.

If you truly want love with a flesh-and-blood person who could love you for who you really are and make love with you for real—that is available. But not if you're hiding out in the fantasy of it.

Are Your Differences Negotiable?

Our intention in this book is to show you how you can make your relationship work, even beyond what you imagined it could be. However, we would be remiss if we did not acknowledge that not all relationships will hold together.

When certain differences between two people are nonnegotiable—for example, he must have children and she is absolutely against it—they cannot stay together. But in all of our work with couples, only rarely have we seen differences so entrenched and hardened that they could not be worked out. That is why we know that with loving dedication to your relationship, you too can resolve your differences to your mutual satisfaction.

Nevertheless, at our trainings and workshops we are invariably asked to highlight some of the issues that can lead to a breakup. Before we do that here, we want to emphasize that your success in handling the most sensitive and challenging differences between you depends on the personal needs, desires, and emotional readiness of each of you to change as your relationship evolves.

Danger Signals

The following danger signals are never, in and of themselves, the kiss of death to a relationship. Rather, they indicate character limitations that, if not addressed with healing lovework, create too much of a burden on an intimate, ongoing, romantic relationship.

Addiction: To the practicing addict, their substance of choice—alcohol, drugs, gambling, sex, whatever—will always come before the relationship. That's not to say that an addict cannot change, but the odds aren't great. Don't get caught believing you'll be so remarkably loving that the addict will divorce their addiction and switch their allegiance to you.

Abuse: When someone is physically and/or emotionally abusive, they are essentially punishing the other person for being different. Couples can work out an elaborate dance of abuse and even call it love. It is not.

Misplaced loyalty: When someone cannot shift their primary loyalty from their family of origin, then the needs, desires, and demands of the new family he or she is co-creating will have to take a backseat. Furthermore, someone whose primary loyalty is to his or her family of origin is in danger of remaining an emotional child.

If a parent gives primary allegiance to children from the current or a previous relationship, then his or her spouse has been relegated to a secondary status for which the relationship and the children will invariably suffer.

Rigidity: Insisting that only certain feelings, beliefs, and behaviors are permissible constitutes emotional rigidity that will prevent a relationship from evolving as it must. Confining a relationship to a predetermined set of rules and obligations demands obedience and denies the possibility of intimacy.

Refusing to talk: When silence dominates a relationship, the opportunity to co-create a life together is foreclosed. Communication is the lifeblood of every successful couple.

Unemployment: A history of unemployment displays a lack of responsibility, an expectation of being taken care of, a fear of being in the world, and/or hatred of authority, to say nothing of the lack of income, which is a burden to any meaningful relationship.

Invisibility: When a person is unwilling to take a position on issues, can't say no, won't reveal feelings, and tries *only* to be pleasant, that is emotional invisibility. There is no one to relate to, so a meaningful relationship cannot be developed.

Secrecy: Keeping silent about the past or future, friends or family, and compartmentalizing the relationship precludes any depth of intimacy.

No commitment: Without the emotional confidence of a future together, there is no possibility for trust. That confidence rests upon a secure and continued commitment.

Possessiveness: As flattering as it might seem initially, a controlling jealousy is born of fear and a lack of confidence. You become an object, locked up in the other's ego.

Fantasy: Someone caught up in romantic fantasy—unrealistic expectations of love, their lover, even themselves—is drifting in the clouds. There is no actual soil for love to grow in.

Finding fault and blaming: When someone can never be satisfied, they are carrying on an emotional affair with their displeasure. They project the cause of their dissatisfaction onto anyone else and blame others for their lot in life. Love cannot compete with that.

Financial instability: Large unsecured debt, and/or no savings/retirement plan in place, points to a significant lack of foresight and self-worth that can bankrupt a relationship.

Unpredictable raging: Rage opens the floodgates of pent-up hurt and aggression, vented on a partner when it should have been directed elsewhere. Rage is usually out of proportion, far beyond what the circumstance warrants. It is a symptom of someone's unaddressed past still dominating his or her life.

Fear of love: Some people crave love but can't feel it and even reject it when it is given to them.

Pretense and performance: If a person is too fearful to reveal themselves for who they are, they have little choice but to pretend. Making a relationship with someone who is always giving a performance can never be satisfying.

Pining: Pining is evidence that someone is attracted to those who are unavailable, or is in love with an ideal of love that is unattainable, or is longing for a caretaker rather than a mate. Although he or she may even be poetic about suffering, that's not someone who can make a real and lasting relationship.

Loving but not liking: The very best marriages are between people who are best friends and lovers. When friendship is absent, then it's not love, but rather something like codependent clinging.

Afraid to be alone/desperate to be with someone: When someone cannot be alone, he or she will become overly dependent on another person to keep from facing the lonely emptiness at the source of their desperation. That does not make for a good relationship.

Obsessing: If someone is trapped in constantly ruminating over, worrying, or fantasizing about the relationship, they are blocked from the reality of what is actually going on.

Sexual cheating: While one indiscretion can be a wake-up call that something needs attention, sexual cheating indicates a compulsive need to make up for poor self-esteem and personal emptiness.

This list is not exhaustive. We're sure you can add more examples. However, we want you to have an idea of the various forms of emotional unavailability that can stand in the way of what you want from love and intimacy.

Keep in mind that these behaviors or attitudes may describe your emotional unavailability as readily as your partner's. It's not uncommon if you find yourself projecting your foibles and less than lovely behaviors onto the one you love in order to avoid taking responsibility for your own blind spots.

Also, it's important to understand that the two of you may have opposing positions with regard to something significant, say the death penalty. But if that isn't relevant to the health and well-being of your relationship, then it is simply grounds for a healthy and fascinating respect for differences.

All of the character traits we've listed can be changed and outgrown. Not one of them will necessarily bring a relationship down by itself, but each can undermine a relationship if the trait is chronic and not addressed and dealt with through healing lovework.

Having read the list, if some of them apply to you and/or your partner, be alert but don't necessarily leap to the conclusion that your relationship won't make it. Others have overcome these issues, and if you are both available for love to be your guide to growth and change, so can you.

How Far Do You Go?

How much should I give? How far should I bend? These are also questions we're asked.

When you're in love and wanting to please your lover, temptation can beckon you to give in, to bend. Your desire to make your partner happy may even cost you your own integrity.

Bending means suppressing your own wants and needs even with issues that are really important to you. That's the same as emotionally disappearing and allowing your partner to have his or her own way.

The problem is that when you continually give in, you are cheating on your relationship by not showing up and letting yourself be known. You are robbing yourself and your partner of who you are. As a result, either you will break under the weight of accumulated resentment or you will snap back in revenge with a force that is tantamount to relationship suicide.

So our answer is very simple. Do not bend at all. Bring *yourself* to the relationship and respectfully resolve the issues that create conflicts between you.

The art of loving conflict resolution is to make certain that what is so important to each of you is recognized and acknowledged. If, in the process of working things out, your partner requests something that doesn't fit for you, you must decline. Then, to keep your love open and alive, explore alternative solutions that will ensure that both of you are seen and heard and that your resolution will be mutually satisfactory to you both and to your relationship.

Don't rush to a settlement just to keep the peace or please your partner. The point is to make sure you are being loved for who you really are—by you as well as by your spouse.

Knowing When to Leave

One more question routinely begs to be answered: How can I know when it's time to leave? There are three specific behaviors that are guaranteed to wreck any chance for lasting love. These are signals that it's time to leave.

Negative Trust

Many relationships are built on what we call *negative trust.* Although joining those two words together may sound like a contradiction, negative trust is very real.

When two people are continually disrespectful and even cruel, they are perpetuating a co-created relationship of negative trust. They can count with certainty on one another's vicious backbiting, sarcasm, contempt, and disgust. Their emotional connection is usually dependent on the predictability of being belittled. This is not love but a morass of dominance and submission, a lost struggle for recognition and respect.

The television series *Married with Children* was an excellent example of an entire family motivated by negative trust. It couldn't have been so popular if abuse weren't so familiar.

If you and your partner continually fall into belittling, controlling, punishing, verbally abusing, and, of course, physically abusing each other, and one or both of you refuses to seek help, that's an obvious signal to leave the relationship.

Nonparticipation

When you realize that you, or your partner, or both of you, are no longer actively participating in the relationship, no longer sincerely curious about each other, no longer interested in nourishing what you have together, that should sound an alarm. No relationship can survive the indifference and neglect of emotional cheating. That's not love but resignation, and it's time to make radical changes or leave.

Imposed Makeovers

Finally, if one or both of you is determined to change the other person, if you are committed to forcing your partner to be a certain way, you're not in love with your partner. You are in love with your own fantasy-lover, an image inside your head. If this is what you're doing, or if it's being done to you, and you can't get your partner to stop or you won't stop, it's time to get out—because, even if you stay together, you'll become resentful and unhappy in the long run.

Remember

The Clash of Differences is not the problem of the Second Passage. It is the treasure. The problem is assuming that the clash shouldn't be happening and then doing whatever you can to stop it. The need for separation is natural. It is the doorway to *knowing* that you can be who you are and be loved through and through. That is a true gift and an absolutely necessary part of the full arc of love.

Exploring
The Clash of Differences

1. Take an inventory of your romantic expectations.

   • What do you imagine a relationship will bring to you?

   • What do you imagine you will have to give back to it?

   • In what ways are you satisfied?

   • In what ways are you disappointed?

   • How does your lover meet your expectations? Have you told him/her?

   • In what ways does your partner fail your expectations? Have you told him/her?

   • In what ways have you met or failed your partner's expectations?

   • Has the Second Passage come as a shock? If so, have you discussed that with your partner?

   The Second Passage is very disturbing to most people. Are you making the mistake of believing that something is wrong and you have to break it off? Or are you willing to dive in and accept the gift, although a demanding one, of this most important passage in the arc of love?

2. To keep your relationship healthy and thriving you must guard against emotional cheating—it can tear the heart out of your relationship. To bring it under control, you must first acknowledge that you are responsible. To begin to do that, answer the following questions:

- Do you go to others for help about your relationship? Do you bring back to your relationship what they advise? If not, why not?

- What is it about confronting your partner that is so frightening? Are you willing to discuss that with him/her? If not, why not?

- What benefit do you imagine would result from keeping your feelings from your partner? What if your partner kept his or her feelings from you?

- Is your partner cheating emotionally as well? If so, how do you feel about that?

- How would you expect your partner to feel if he/she discovered you were cheating emotionally?

- What is the payoff for you to be an emotional cheater? There must be a payoff or you wouldn't be doing it.

Your answers to these questions will help you begin the process of committing more concretely to your relationship. If your relationship is young, don't starve it to death. If you've been together awhile, make amends for the wounds caused by emotional cheating.

3. It is important to balance the tension of the Second Passage with a vision of what is possible as you continue to mature. Consider all the ways your relationship is terrific even now. Use that as a basis for imagining what it will be like once you pass through this time of identity separation. It is essential that you and your partner continue to talk about how you cherish each other, how you respect each other, and how you want to build upon these feelings of love and confidence.

CHAPTER TEN

The Principles:
The Alchemical Power of Two

*W*hile the Second Passage is an exasperating time, it is also an essential time in the course of love's arc. And though that could be said about any of the four passages, none are so predictive of the future as is *The Clash of Differences* and how each of you responds.

The First Passage is a bit like *getting* pregnant. It's thrilling and exciting. The Second Passage is like *being* pregnant. Sometimes you're worried, anxious. She doesn't know if she can be a good mother. He realizes he will be the only source of financial support. You might even feel sick to your stomach. She's sick in the morning, he's sick at night. Things are changing at such a quick pace. Then you're back to being elated and thrilled, and the emotional and physical roller-coaster ride continues.

Just as being pregnant is a precarious time for the developing child—will the baby develop normally? will it come to term?—so too is the Second Passage of love. Will you allow love to grow normally so that both of you can feel loved for all that you are? Will you surrender to what love needs from you and allow your relationship to make it all the way?

These principles can help you make the most of *The Clash of Differences.*

The Clash Is Unavoidable

No matter how much you have in common, it's inevitable that you will have differing and sometimes clashing opinions, feelings, and behaviors. You will hurt each other's feelings, not because you want to but because you can't avoid being different and banging into one another from time to time.

Laurie and Denny LeClear are good friends of ours. They were married for five years, then divorced. After two years apart, they remarried. That was ten years ago. They now run the LeClear Connection in Kalamazoo, Michigan, where they teach relationship classes.

They give an example from their first go-around of what they did when either of them would get sick and how they did not recognize, let alone value, their differences.

Laurie loved to be pampered and nursed, tucked into bed and fed chicken soup. So when Denny was sick that's how she would treat him. It was her way of loving him. He hated it! Why? Because when he was sick he just wanted to be left alone. So when Laurie wasn't feeling well, that's what he did to show his love for her. He left her alone. She hated it!

Although it's hard to believe, they never talked about it at all. They just suffered in silence. That particular problem was added in with everything else they couldn't help clashing over—how Laurie made social plans for them without asking Denny, how he would try to ignore problems like a bank account being overdrawn. Having no idea how to learn from each other, they were forced to do what so many couples do, even couples whose love is sincere. They divorced.

What made the difference between the first marriage and the second? While they were apart they continued to communicate. In doing so, they realized that they needed to talk about their different backgrounds, their personal preferences, and their different ways of loving. The only way their relationship could have a chance was if they revealed who they really were as they went along.

So, one way or the other, *The Clash of Differences* is unavoidable. Not in every moment, just some of the time. If you're not there yet, expect it. If you're in it, know that it's necessary for the development of each of you as individuals and as a couple. If you're in a long-term relationship and you keep avoiding it by holding your tongue or rationalizing your spouse's behavior, please stop cheating on your relationship. Open up. You don't have to yell and scream, though most people do fall into fighting every now and then.

Take comfort in the fact that this change in your relationship is inevitable and invaluable. It is part of the natural arc of love.

Both of You Count

As we've said, in the First Passage the oneness is sublime. In the Second Passage, your *twoness*—the realities of two distinct individuals—is required to further the growth of love.

Living Together

Even if it's your first date, you are living those hours of your lives *together*. When you share a household, you are living *together* as a full-time commitment. It's your undeveloped emotional, psychological, and spiritual *together* that the Second Passage exposes—and must expose in order for you to see what is problematic between you. Only then can you learn new skills to support your day-to-day *together*. Only then can you create what is needed to make your specific twoness satisfying and deeply meaningful.

Your Specific Twoness

Your relationship can be like no one else's. It has to be made out of what each of you needs and wants, and what feels right given each of your family backgrounds, life experiences, and future goals. So both of you must participate and shape your togetherness together. That's the only way love can be given a dwelling place that is both balanced and safe.

When you start experiencing *The Clash of Differences*, whether it's the first time, or later when you least expect it, keep in mind that it can't be resolved on anyone else's terms, not even those of a counselor, unless those terms work for both of you. Remember that you are being brought along by your souls' insistence that you both expand. Your expansion must include one another—not merely follow a prescribed format developed by someone else.

An intimate relationship is a work of art, and the Second Passage is the process of getting all your colors onto the palette so you have a full spectrum with which to paint. And just like a real palette, some of the colors will clash as they sit next to each other. But once you both start applying your paints, dabbing, feathering, and blending your colors onto the canvas with your own unique brushes and in just the right ways that harmonize with one another's vision, then voila—magic occurs! Shadings and hues previously unimagined begin to reveal themselves. A depth and dimension of spirit emerges through your painting.

So too for your specific behavioral, emotional, psychological, sexual, and spiritual differences, once you learn how to paint your own special togetherness instead of trying to imitate anyone else's.

The Alchemical Power of Consciousness

That *The Clash of Differences* is alchemical is not merely a metaphor. It is real. It changes emotional lead into emotional gold. So you must be ready to be changed by being loved, and you must be ready to be changed by loving someone.

The Second Passage introduces you to the ongoing lovework necessary to infuse your relationship with an ever-growing and ever-changing, co-created landscape. Through lovework you experience the alchemical power of fire, a flame ignited by two different people, each committed to their being together, that transforms old fears and beliefs into new freedoms, new awareness, new life!

Lovework

By lovework we mean the attention and care both of you must give to putting forth your grievances, hurts, and requests for change. It is listening to one another when you crash into a conflict, hearing the other side of things with curiosity and as much compassion as your own anger and/or hurt will allow. It is the process of resolving your differences to your mutual satisfaction and for the benefit of your relationship.

We can already hear some of you protesting, "But you shouldn't have to work at love!"

That's totally unrealistic. When two distinctly different people join their lives together it always takes consciously loving effort to work through the rough spots and heal the hurt feelings.

The beauty and blessings of lovework come to you because, in the process, you are always learning more about yourself and each other. You are pressed by one another's needs to find new ways to relate with each other. You get to see the world from the other's perspective. You are expanded and opened to co-create something that has never before existed until you began blending your lives into being a couple.

The more commitment and care you give to your lovework, the more fulfilling your relationship will be.

Conflict Is Healthy

It's not conflict that is dangerous, it's how you think about it and how you manage it that can lead to danger. When we speak of conflict we're not referring to dirty fighting in which the goal is to defeat the other person and stand victorious over a smashed relationship. What good is that? And don't leap to the conclusion that you're not well-matched just because you see things differently or you've hurt each other.

If that's what you believe, you're stuck in the illusion that love will always be effortless and discomfort-free. That's a fantasy and has nothing to do with love or real life.

Your conflicts offer the opportunity to grasp the intense importance of your lover's hurt feelings or the value of a certain behavior or attitude that clashes with yours. Without overt, expressed conflict, you may never know the full impact of your own distinctiveness. Without the truth of your separate identities, you can never know enough about each other to feel the compassionate love that inspires the desire to find new ways of being together that will suit you both.

Dis-illusionment Is Necessary

For there to be room for each of you in your relationship, the initial "stars in your eyes" blindness of love will have to give way to the actual reality of who you are. That will be disillusioning, guaranteed!

Initially, dis-illusionment is no fun. But it is an eyeopener. If you cannot love one another with your eyes wide open, with full awareness of the blessings and limitations each of you brings to real romance, then you can never trust the love you say you feel.

When you enter the Second Passage, you've stepped onto the ground of an initiation. You are being called to consciousness and initiated into the spiritual purpose of your romantic relationship. One of the first tests is whether or not you can stand the discomfort of dis-illusionment.

If you approach it willing to learn, you will see that in the arc of love the illusions you hold about your partner and about yourself must be burned away so you can clearly see who it is you claim to love, who you are as a loving partner, and what it actually means to be committed. If you cannot bear this process, or if you discover that you do not love the other person once your blinders are off, you will break up. That's a success. The tragedy would be if you remained together and spent the rest of your days in a loveless relationship, badgering one another to change, trapped in the illusion that you can go back to how it used to be in the beginning.

Cutting through Self-Centeredness

Within *The Clash of Differences* there is another kind of blindness that will be exposed and must be faced—the precious illusion that only your way is the right way. It's called unhealthy narcissism. For you to pursue what love wants for you, you will need to step down off your throne of self-importance. And lo and behold, what does the Universe supply to help you do the job? A partner who won't put up with you trying to hog the show.

Now don't resist by saying, "Well, it doesn't apply to me. I'm totally giving and always think of the other person first." You no doubt think that's being selfless. But that's just another form of narcissism in which you're taken with your saintly qualities, whether anyone wants them or not. The same holds true for those of you who think you are always the most inadequate, the most unpopular, the most unattractive or unsuccessful. You are simply using the reverse as the way you stand apart in your special, self-centered lowliness.

The truth is, each one of us has a dose of unhealthy narcissism threatening to undermine our ability to join our lives with someone else's. When we open to the pressure of the Second Passage, we are expanded so that we can be more aware of the one we say we love, and truly value the otherness of this person we want to be with.

Love will show you there really is someone out there who counts as much as you do. And then, whoa! You're not the center of everything. What you were supposed to learn in kindergarten you'll learn now: You have to share. Otherwise you will never be able to truly care or be cared for.

Far from Home

Over the last one hundred years, radical changes have emerged in what men and women believe about courtship and romance, and those changes have happened faster than ever before in history. Today we have almost limitless personal freedom to choose our mate and co-create the lifestyle we want to live. When it comes to who and how we love, we are bursting with expectations of individual freedom and personal responsibility, and we're having to deal with it in ways that men and women have never had to before.

Furthermore, people are freer to move, to leave the area of their birth in search of the life and love they envision. That leaves us challenged to make relationships with partners who were raised differently and often come from backgrounds that may include cultural, racial, religious, political, educational, and socio-economic differences. So the issue of differences—how we deal with them, what we learn from them, what changes they demand of us, what we expect in return—is more crucial than ever before.

Where Is Your Allegiance?

Many of the values you hold were formed at the time and place of your childhood. That's true for all of us. They are part of your back story. And some part of you is still dedicated to beliefs that worked for you at the time and in the place you formed them. But, as Dorothy said in *The Wizard of Oz,* "We're not in Kansas anymore, Toto." Things have changed, and perhaps radically.

Don't be surprised when *The Clash of Differences* brings to the surface all manner of allegiances and loyalties to the ideals of your family and their ways of being. You may find yourselves fighting not about what really matters to the two of you, but about whose family had the right or better way to celebrate a holiday, cut a turkey, go camping, raise a child, balance a checkbook, or praise God. When that happens, you are faced with a question. Where is your allegiance? To the family you came from or the one are co-creating?

If intimacy is what you want, then you must let go of some, not all, of what you thought before you committed to the co-creation of your future. You must make space inside you for your new family to come to life. Your soul is leading now, and you'll be asked to make new loyalties. You can do that by making sure your partner means more to you than your attachment to the habits and customs of where you came from. Then you will free yourself for this new adventure, one that is larger, more creative, and far more generative than what you've previously known.

You Will Get Lost

The word *familiar* has the same root as the word *family*. An attraction to someone is, in part, your attraction to what is familiar. That's understandable. It's both comfortable and comforting.

But as the relationship deepens, you will be exposed more and more to that which is *not* familiar, *not* family. Sometimes you will feel lost. That doesn't mean you *are* lost. In fact, you are on your way to finding yourself more fully than ever before. But you will have to let go of some of what has been with you since you were very young and over which you had no choice. You will have to let it go forever because it belonged to the environment of your youth, and love requires your maturity.

For example, someone born into a poverty-stricken family had no choice but to experience poverty. Or someone born into an alcoholic family had no choice but to deal with the turmoil that alcoholism inflicts. Even someone born into wealth and privilege had no choice. You might not think that would be such a problem, but everything comes with a price. Each of us is socialized in a specific psychological and spiritual circumstance that limits who we think we are and what we think we can have.

In the Second Passage you can now consciously and assertively assume the power of your own identity. For a time, you may feel adrift, guilty, confused, lost. That's because you've been inspired to desire love rather than to be "right," "good," or "acceptable." In other words, you have opened to be more of who you are instead of staying in allegiance to beliefs and ambitions that were adaptive in your family but no longer work.

Love insists that you move out of what has been so familiar and move into the unknown. And now, perhaps for the first time, with the help of your lover, you get to discover and know yourself for the truth that reaches down through your heart into the wisdom of your soul.

Where's the Humor in This?

The Second Passage is so often messy and confusing that it really helps to have a sense of humor. Once in a while you need to be able to laugh at yourself and even at the situation.

Judith: After I'd filed a few serious complaints about Jim being self-centered at my expense—meaning he ignored something I'd said or made a plan without consulting me, that kind of thing—I started teasing him about "The Big N." That *N* stood for "narcissism." Because I was able to laugh, he was more receptive and now it's become a way to joke with him when he gets caught up in himself.

Jim: You've heard the story of the princess and the pea. The princess was so sensitive she could be kept awake by the irritation of one pea placed beneath a stack of mattresses. Well, Judith is very sensitive. When we were first together I thought she was being melodramatic. Now, rather than challenge her, I just ask, "Where's the pea?" That question has become an endearment which helps us regain perspective when things get tense.

We weren't able to joke about these things right away. But as we progressed through the Second Passage and grew to trust that we really were allies, we could make humor part of the real romance of our relationship.

Not a Straight Line

Don't expect the arc of love to be a straight-line process. Aspects of each passage may show up at any time. In the middle of the tension of the Second Passage, you can be swept away by powerful and abandoned First Passage sex. Or during the curiosity that is essential to the Third Passage, in a moment of almost clairvoyant brilliance, you may see the grandeur of the Fourth Passage and be humbled by the awesome closeness that is growing between you.

The further along in the process, the more emotionally skilled you will be and the more trust you will have to see you through whatever comes up.

Exploring
The Clash of Differences

1. Because conflict, especially fighting, takes place in the wilderness of your relationship, you can't see things clearly. You may be afraid of being overrun. That's when you may need your anger to support you, to help you assert your point of view, and in that way take care of yourself.

   It's true that many people are frightened by anger, believing that it can only do damage. But, like any powerful force, that all depends on how you use it. Rather than avoid it, by understanding the value of anger you can turn it into a trustworthy ally.

   Anger alerts you that your personal boundaries have been crossed. By accepting anger as a legitimate and healthy response to certain events, you can rely on it to prevent yourself from being mistreated.

   Anger can help you ask, if not demand, that your complaints and concerns be respected. By helping you to make yourself clear, anger is a positive power that benefits both you and your partner.

   Anger can unblock bound-up tensions, freeing you to fully express your view of the conflict. When you trust anger, it can release you to reveal more and more of yourself, which is what any conflict requires if you are to arrive at a mutually beneficial resolution.

By expressing anger, you learn that you need not be afraid of it. Even more so, you learn that if you express your anger with discernment and respect, it serves as a laser beam, cutting through distortion and honing in on what is really at issue. Anger can be like a scalpel, cutting away obstacles to growth and deeper intimacy.

Healthy, respectful anger is part of a truly spiritual relationship. It is often the source of a profound resolve to take a new look at what you have co-created, opening your future to even greater possibilities.

2. When you notice that you've been biting your tongue and biding your time with some complaint in order to keep the peace or not hurt the other's feelings, always reveal it as soon as you can. Then talk about why it felt so dangerous to speak up. This can lead you to a mutual agreement about how to bring up difficult issues more easily in the future.

3. Remind yourselves, whenever a conflict arises, that the goal is always to reach an outcome that improves your lives individually and together. To get there you have to remember that each of you has a piece of the present-time emotional truth between you, and a piece of emotional baggage or distortion that's helping to throw everything out of kilter. If there were no distortion you would not be struggling.

Consequently, you need each other if you are going to reach a mutually satisfactory resolution. You are both right, according to your own present-time experience, feelings, interests, and values. Therefore both of your truths must be recognized.

You are also both wrong, in that you are blind to your own emotionally inflamed distortions which are triggered by old wounds, fears, and sensitivities. Each distortion must be faced and dissolved.

Helping each other to recognize the distortions but not blaming one another for the upsets and changes that are taking place can lead you to fuller trust, deepened intimacy, and richly successful conflict resolution.

Practice resolving your differences in ways that respect and honor both of you. This will take more time and energy than just giving in to keep the peace, or allowing one of you to dictate how it will be.

But the outcome will be so sweet, because you'll both know you are loved enough to be granted a full hearing on whatever you're disagreeing over, hurting over, or fighting over. And remember—each of you is worth the lovework it takes to discover what will make a better future.

CHAPTER ELEVEN

The Payoff:
Love in Flesh and Blood

When you enter the Second Passage of love's arc, it's easy to miss the payoffs for all the difficulties. But because you never learned any other way, it's just a problem of consciousness. There is an alternative, one that allows you to see how blessed you are to encounter one another in all your glorious and not so glorious differences.

Think of it this way, love has gone fishing for more of you and sent your lover to throw out the lure. In response, deeply buried facets of your personality are enlivened and come out of hiding. Now more of you is available to love. Love has also sent you to provide just the lure your lover needs to become more available for love.

Because the Second Passage is a particularly challenging time, it is vitally important that you know the spiritual purpose of *The Clash of Differences* is to open you to be you, all of you, and make sure you are loved for being just that. If you're with someone who cannot love you as you are, you get to find out. That's a successful discovery of the truth!

You also get to learn whether or not you love your lover for who he or she really is. You may discover that what you feel as love is really your response to your images and fantasies of love and not for the full reality of the person you're with. The Second Passage will push you to dig deeper into the meaning and experience of being with a flesh-and-blood person and to leave behind the false notion of romance you've mistaken for love.

The purpose for the struggles of the Second Passage is to burn away your illusions so that you really get it that the only way you can fail is by pursuing that which is not love.

A Time of Wholeness

It's very likely that your family wasn't well-equipped to embrace you as you were, and they weren't able to fully support the growth and development of your uniqueness. For some of you, their failure was miserable. They were too uninformed and too caught up in their own problems.

Now you are responsible for living as an expression of your wholeness. Now you have a soul-supported chance for establishing your identity on your own terms, more expansively and expressively than ever before. Now you can come forth and be revealed for your truest worth, your weirdest quirks, your goofiest humor, your darkest broodings . . . whatever makes you you! That's one part of the payoff present in the alchemical magic of *The Clash of Differences.*

Your Soul Is Forcing Your Hand

Whether you can feel it or not, you have deep inner support driving you into and through the Second Passage. Your soul wants you to grow and thrive as it calls you to unveil your self.

Your insecurities may beg you to bolt, but an inner voice prevents you from backing out.

That voice urges you to see what is right about all this confusion. It keeps you focused and noticing that with each uncomfortable encounter somehow the two of you feel even closer, more willing to trust that something special is going on. Your soul protects you from acting out your fear and encourages you to learn more about how love actually works.

You Are Being Made Available

No one is fully prepared for what love will require from them. It's only when you're in the fire that you will discover much about yourself that you hadn't anticipated. That doesn't mean you shouldn't prepare. It does mean you will have to give yourself some slack when you come up against the lessons you couldn't see coming.

We are all self-involved to one degree or another and are blind to what may be right in front of us. That's why the challenges in your differences are so critical. They compel you to open your emotional and spiritual eyes and see more of reality. When you don't, you deny your partner's distinctiveness and, not surprisingly, you deny your own. There's no room for anything but what you've already decided is real and right. When there is no room for discovery, there is no love.

One of the most powerful payoffs of the Second Passage is confronting your insistence, conscious or not, that only you count, only your way is the right way. Your soul attracts you to your lover, with his or her differences as a catalyst, to open you to the wisdom of love. You are yanked out of your insulated world and ushered into the larger human community where you will have to live with someone else—someone who is an *other,* not like you. Though it may not seem so at first, the payoff is huge, because it makes you available to truly enjoy the very love and loving you want.

Your Lover's Dark Underbelly

Love isn't an archaeological dig into just your psyche. Your lover gets dug into as well. Conflicts do that. They work to penetrate surface disguises where never-healed emotional wounds are still raw. Once exposed, they can't be denied. That is sure to overturn some of what you expected and it may even frighten you.

Judith: When we met, Jim lived at the beach in Marina del Rey, California, and drove a Mercedes. One of his first gifts to me, which I still have, was a gorgeous blue Italian-knit sweater from a posh store in Los Angeles. Sounds like he was set financially, right? Wrong. As we became more and more serious, I learned that he had a love/hate relationship with his personal finances, and even avoided balancing his checkbook because it made him so anxious.

Jim: For all of Judith's professional success as a model/actress earlier in her life and as a clinical psychologist when we met, it turned out that she was deeply fearful. When we moved in together she insisted on installing high-security Medico locks on every door, and she could not sleep with the windows open—on the second floor! Yet to the world she appeared poised and assured.

Judith: As surprising as these underbelly elements were, we were committed to discovering the full truth of our experiences and helping one another work through and transform them.

When you decide you can live with and love one another, emotional baggage included, then you can convert these dark, pain-filled elements into life-affirming intimacy when you move into the Third Passage. If you cannot, do not stay together abusing one another and adding unnecessary pain to what you've already experienced.

But please remember that no matter what it feels like and no matter what you imagine your lover should have told you right from the start—about his or her neurotic fears, difficult loyalties to still-living parents, obsessive connections with grown children, whatever it may be—you have not been betrayed. Part of what an intimate committed relationship does is root out unconscious material, some of which we're not even aware of until it appears.

Are You a Worthy Dwelling Place for Love?

In the First Passage, just like in Eden, everything was provided for you. You were swept up and given to and it was effortless. Now you are on your own. Love has deepened and you need to find out if you can follow its unfolding invitation.

Do you have enough of your own sense of self to stand separate and engage in the clashes when your differences collide? Are you willing to make yourself available to be further strengthened and clarified as a distinct and unique self? Do you recognize the Second Passage as a spiritual basis for real-life love? Do you accept and respect that both of you are expressions of the wondrous diversity of life, neither one more important nor more right than the other?

The rigors of the Second Passage provide the opportunity to discover yourself as truly capable of love. It is a journey through your heartfelt commitment and devotion, to live a life that continually asks for more and pays off in kind. It's your chance to stake your claim to love, pronouncing yourself ready, willing, and able to proceed along its full arc.

You Must Leave Home

In the Book of Genesis, God commands Abraham, "Leave thy country, thy kinsmen and thy father's house and go unto a land I will show thee and I will make of thee a new nation." Notice, however, that if God were being merely a tour guide, His instruction would have been the other way around—"Leave thy father's house, thy kinsmen and thy country." But Abraham was not receiving a travel schedule, he was receiving a spiritual command.

Abraham had to first break his allegiance to his country, the easiest of his loyalties; then to his kinsmen, his immediate community of neighbors and extended family; and then to his father's house, the most difficult loyalty to release, and only then was he worthy of opening to a new life.

The same applies to love and relationship. You must let go of being your parents' good boy or girl. If not, you will remain a child, not able to co-create your own family as you see fit. In short, you must grow up and grow into your own mind, body, and soul.

Whether you make it through the Second Passage as a loving couple depends not only on how you respond to the challenges before you, but also on whether you are mature enough to switch your loyalty to your new life. You will never know the depth of connection available between you if you feel compelled to impose on the relationship your beliefs and values from another time and place that are not applicable to the two of you. If you are going to achieve the kind of connection and commitment that spiritually generative love needs, your new family must gain your primary allegiance.

The Clash of Differences provides the opportunity for you to incorporate an entirely other person into your lifestyle, into your heart, into what makes life more meaningful for you. That will certainly cause each of you to leave behind some, but not all, of what you've previously cherished.

Establishing Trust

It's very tempting to imagine that when you meet the "right one," you will immediately be able to trust one another completely. But not so. Genuine trust is always earned, and it must be earned from three directions. You must be able to trust yourself, you must be a trustworthy partner, and you must discover to what extent your partner can be trusted.

It takes the Second Passage to determine if you can trust yourself in the relationship. You are tested to see if you will show up and stake your claim for what you need, how you feel, what you want to see changed. You also see your own weaknesses and limitations, where you need to grow and develop, and what the relationship needs from you if it is going to make it.

Tanasha and Rasheed had been married for five years when they came to see us. Rasheed had been noisy and resistant since he was a little kid. He was often punished for being a trouble-maker. When they were first married, if he felt Tanasha wasn't listening to him with her full attention, he saw that as disrespect and would blow up.

Tanasha would erupt right back and they would end up fighting the way her father and mother had fought—mean and ugly.

Neither one wanted to hurt the other, but they were caught in a pattern they couldn't control. Rasheed felt unheard and Tanasha felt attacked.

After we pointed out the roots of their pattern, we showed them that they could use loving curiosity to learn more about one another's hurt and fear. They practiced listening respectfully and agreed to talk to each other about their problem when they weren't emotionally embroiled in it.

They realized that both of their responses were way out of balance and they were surprised to discover just how well-matched they were to provoke each other's reactions.

They had to leave their allegiances to family patterns behind and join together more effectively. Tanasha had to learn how to fight back more powerfully and Rasheed had to learn to let go of his attachment to what he thought it was to be a man.

We encouraged and supported them in developing the emotional skills they needed to both feel listened to and loved. They finally came to see how their recurring fight was a blessing in disguise, as they learned to trust themselves and one another more and more.

Now they can both be angry, and they can both be sensitive and compassionate. Having learned to deal with this potentially marriage-breaking issue, they trust that they can work out anything that comes up between them.

The bottom line of trust is revealed in *The Clash of Differences*. Do you feel safe disclosing who you are, who you really are? Are your differences met with curiosity and respect?

Don't turn a blind eye to all the signals that your partner is not trustworthy—he doesn't do what he says he will, she lies to you, he refuses to talk about his past, she snoops through your mail, he borrows money and doesn't repay you, she repeatedly breaks dates with you, and so on.

We're not talking about *one* offense. You must pay attention to *patterns* of deceit or lack of personal responsibility. Please do the lovework of confronting your lover about the untrustworthy behavior and insist that it be changed. If that happens—success! If it doesn't happen, or if your partner denies any wrongdoing, please trust yourself and leave the relationship. Success!

Remember, love wants more of you and it sent your lover to draw you out. In response, deeply buried facets of your personality are enlivened and come out of hiding. Now more of you is available to love. And love has also sent you as exactly what is needed to draw your lover out so that he or she can be more revealing, alive, and available as well.

Something Bigger

The Second Passage opens the gateway for a love that is much, much larger and deeper than that in the First Passage.

Is it messy? Sure.

More difficult? Yes, indeed.

Worth it? Absolutely, if what you want is a love that will last a lifetime.

Be aware that you can never fail, even if you break up or divorce, as long as you continually learn to trust yourself. Like everything else, self-awareness and practice are necessary.

Both men and women are susceptible to losing themselves in a relationship. They may be competent and secure in their business and among their friends, but as soon as they get romantically involved with someone all of that can disappear.

She loses sight of what she wants from her life and does whatever he says. "I can't trust myself to say no to sex," she complains. "When I'm around him I do whatever he decides."

He can't trust himself to voice his complaints. "So I go and shoot hoops with my buddies. It's amazing, I'm not afraid of them, but she scares me to death."

So it's important that you work to trust yourself more and more. Here are the goals to keep in mind:

Trust yourself to show up.

Trust yourself to object when you are being mistreated.

Trust yourself to ask for what you want.

Trust yourself to acknowledge when your partner is earnest in wanting to change.

Trust yourself to determine when you are being manipulated.

Trust yourself to hold your own in a conflict.

And trust yourself to value the quality of your actual being together over your illusion of "how it's supposed to be."

Exploring
The Clash of Differences

1. Show affection for your tricky, annoying, hard-to-change, or nonnegotiable differences. Give them nicknames. Lovingly joke about them. That way you can feel some affection for your lover without letting go of your very real annoyance.

Judith: I call Jim "The Ditz" when he is the absent-minded professor.

Jim: I call Judith "PPS" (for Pigpen Sherven) when she's eating leftovers not because she's enjoying them but out of an old loyalty to her family's obsession with never wasting food.

Judith: Early on, when Jim would leave the toilet seat up, I'd let him know I was annoyed.

Jim: So whenever I used the toilet with the seat up, and Judith was nearby, I'd shout out, "Can you hear this?" Then I'd drop the seat with a bang. She'd laugh with appreciation and I had fun doing it. After a while, it became an endearment for us.

Some differences are not responsive to cute names and gestures and must be treated with appropriate concern. But when you can, lighten up and let your affection lead. That makes things much easier and much more loving.

2. Invent a ritual to acknowledge and celebrate each successfully resolved clash of differences. It may just be a special "hey babe, we did great" with a warm hug. Or you could give yourselves an IOU for ice cream at your favorite place when the time is right. The point is to stay alert to the payoffs of the Second Passage as a way of mining its precious treasure.

3. As an ongoing topic of significant intimacy, discuss how your differences are stretching you to change, expanding your spiritual awareness, moving you to see yourselves and one another more honestly. These conversations need to be held when you are feeling close and connected with one another.

    Be sure not to condemn where either of you has come from or use this as a time to lecture on what still needs to change. You are being very vulnerable and intimate—keep your hearts open and celebrate how you are letting love lead you home to yourselves and to a love you can trust with your whole heart and soul.

The Third Passage

The Magic of Differences
Two Become Three

CHAPTER TWELVE

The Passion:
All the Ways You Are

*W*hen you truly grasp the fact that you and your spouse are different, and that your differences are what make each of you who you are, an entirely new and wondrous dimension opens in your being together.

We recently received the following email letter from Fasoto Olu, a man from Lagos, Nigeria, and a subscriber to our weekly newsletter. He is thirty-five and his wife, Dupe, is thirty-four. He works in a commercial bank and she is a teacher working for the government of Nigeria. They have three children, two boys and a girl.

He told us that their relationship was a happy romance from the beginning because his sister must have taught Dupe about his likes and dislikes. But after marriage, he said, life was almost a hell, because their differing interests blew up. But things have changed, as his response to us clearly indicates.

I am filled with joy all over. In the bus, train, car, office, church just name it (everywhere) I am happier now. This joy has been derived through Jesus Christ who made it possible for me to come in contact with your programme. My relationship is now rich in love. You see what I mean, i.e. we now trust each other absolutely due to your teachings on interactive communication between husband and wife.

When I came across your newsletter it was a big lesson. I ran home to my wife with copies of your writings and she saw determination in me that I love her. Oh my God, she got determined to make things work too.

Reading your newsletter, there and then we discussed our likes and dislikes. The resultant effect is that during the process we discovered that our earlier misunderstandings were borne out of genuine love for each other. But lack of communication killed the inner light.

Tradition does not even help us as it was the practice from our local villages that only men should have a say in all things. There was not much respect accorded women's opinion. Even Higher College Education does not break this bad old habit. However, when I adopted your problem solving pills (open hearted communication with one's partner – taking into consideration the timing, mood/circumstance, and convenience to both parties) it seemed I've just re-discovered my self. I now know who I am. Oh! one can be miserable without understanding what is happening around him.

We thought we didn't love each other, whereas it wasn't so, rather we were expecting too much from each other.

Today we like to involve ourselves in things like donations to the church, visiting schools to see who we can help financially even as we are just growing up our financial base. These are our life ambitions and we felt we shouldn't wait until we become super millionaires. Identification of Life Interests, we call it. Man does it bring joy.

We now discuss freely all issues including differences and our perception of life and our ambitions and why we have chosen such. I now love to respect my wife and in turn she adores me. Whaoh. It's simply wonderful. Can you imagine!!! She is now very anxious that I come home on time and good/sweet food awaits my arrival from work daily. Honestly, it's like we've just wedded. Thanks a lot.

From your subscriber friend,
Fasoto Olu, Lagos, Nigeria

The Gateway to Lasting Romance

The three questions we're most often asked are:

How do you keep romance alive?

How do you make a relationship last?

How do you make sex exciting over the years?

There's no disputing that partners find it difficult to sustain their excitement for one another. Children, household routines, careers, and whatever reticence or inexperience they bring to their being together wears them down.

Far too many couples never get beyond the pressures of the Second Passage. They resign, figuring there's nothing more they can do to make it better, nothing more they can have. They descend into emotional remote control or they fall into chronic fighting because at least then they can feel something. Or they divorce, hoping to do it differently the next time. They're trying their best to cope with what has become unmanageable.

But there is good news. Very, very good news—you don't have to do that. You don't have to settle. You don't have to flee. You don't have to watch love die.

The main test of the Second Passage—recognizing your self-centeredness by learning to appreciate and resolve your differences to benefit both of you—brings you to the next threshold, the Third Passage in the arc of love, *The Magic of Differences.*

Now you begin to see your differences for the brilliant gems they are. The fun you have together, your ongoing learning and personal growth, even your worldly successes are all enhanced by the magical intersection of your differences.

Your love is ever more delightful as you come to know yourselves and one another more fully through your differences. Love flourishes anew, sprouting new expressions, new colors, new opportunities. Romance is limited only by your imagination and your ability to receive what is given to you. The power and passion of sex evolves into lovemaking, with its deeper honesty and deeper dedication to satisfying your personal and spiritual needs as well as your biological desires.

The very same differences that, not too long ago, were driving you crazy, become the stuff of incredible connection, discovery, awe, humor, and play.

Your differences now serve as the gateway to the thrilling openness and the ongoing real-life romance of your future together.

Congratulations! You have entered *The Magic of Differences.*

Embracing *The Magic of Differences*

How do you keep passion and romance alive? It's in the differences—in all the ways you and the one you love bring your different points of view to what you are co-creating. After all, what can "co-create" mean if there aren't two of you, with your own specific contributions?

As you read this, you may still be caught up in the struggles of the Second Passage and any thought of embracing your partner's perspective may sound like emotional suicide. Okay, we understand. But as long as you persist and learn to hear each other out—with care and respect—you are going deeper into the heart of love. Like Fasoto and Dupe, you discover the treasure that is waiting there.

It's a New Time

Because we've all learned to fear those who are not like us, we worry that those others will judge us as "stupid," "out of line," "too much." So we've learned to stay at a distance, emotionally remote and isolated from others and, like it or not, from ourselves. That's what kills romance and passion—the distance we keep, especially from the special person we want to live with and who we claim to love.

Fortunately, it's a new time in human consciousness. Old ways of thinking about differences are being seen as crude and maladaptive. Diversity, representing the value of different points of view, has recently gained greater appreciation and a growing legitimacy. Because of the media, especially television and the Internet, we know too much about others to merely discount them out of hand. That kind of knee-jerk prejudice has come under intense scrutiny and has lost much of its power to be persuasive. A new and powerful awareness has opened in human consciousness, shrinking the world into a virtual neighborhood and forever changing the way we think and the way we live.

What does that have to do with keeping romance alive? Well, at the core of this change in awareness is the realization that each and every one of us is a miracle, a unique expression of the magic of Creation. Each and every one of us counts.

For you to grasp the fullness of your own and your partner's experience, you must find your way to understand and respect each other as singular, separate, and distinct expressions of human life. That's practical spirituality, great romance, and *The Magic of Differences*!

No More Conflicts?

Does that mean your differences will never again trigger conflict or anger? Not at all. Now both of you are even more alive in your complexity and you're bound to crash into each other from time to time.

However, as you advance into the third and fourth passages, you keep turning emotional hot spots into productive points for exploration as you become more and more skilled at digging for the meaning buried in your difficulties, more and more confident of the value available when you persist. You learn to cherish the freedom that follows when an old wound, an old confusion, an old longing is unraveled, understood, and released. You both enjoy more emotional freedom in your relationship and more psychological space to be who you are. Blame becomes childish, responsibility becomes a blessing, and it doesn't matter which of you ignited the conflict, you both know there is healing at hand within the tension of the moment.

In the Third Passage the point is to use your challenges to enrich your relationship by gaining the freedom to reveal and celebrate your talents and excellence, as well as to welcome the opportunity to bring your private, dark corners into the light of your love.

You Are Two Different People

The only way to truly experience respect and love for someone is to understand and cherish that he or she is not you. Accepting this truth, rather than resisting it by trying to get your partner to be just like you, is fundamental to the success of your relationship.

"Of course," you say, "I'm standing here, he's over there. I'm female, he's male. I'm wearing blue, he's in brown. It's so obvious. What's your point?" Well, it's not as obvious as it seems.

Have you ever been in a relationship where the other person was trying to control you, trying to get you to behave in some way they wanted? When we ask this question at our workshops, everyone raises their hand.

Have you ever been in a relationship where you were trying to control the other person? All hands go up again, this time with the laughter of guilty admission.

In both instances, the idea that *the other person is not you* doesn't apply, except physically. Psychologically, you wipe your partner out by not truly recognizing him or her. You consciously or unconsciously refuse to grant them their rightful status as an *other*, an other who is different.

Have you ever complained to a friend about your lover, saying, "He should have known"? Or, "Well, I would have done it differently." Or, "She shouldn't have to be told what I like." Or you've said to a friend, "Well, no wonder you got in trouble. I would never have done that." Or, "I can't believe you just said that." In every example, the only reference point is you. Only your world matters. The other person is irrelevant. You don't really know that the other person is not you!

You are unique. So is your partner. At the heart of sincere and lasting love is the respect and value you give to one another and to yourselves—a real, day-to-day practice of celebrating and acknowledging that the other person is *not* you. That's how you discover the alchemical magic at the heart of your differences, the kind of magic that makes each of you and your connection more complete, more whole, and more holy.

The Opposite Sex? Really?

What is opposite about the so-called opposite sex?

The word *opposite* comes from the same root as the word *opponent:* to be set against another. But we are not biologically opposed. We are complementary to one another—mutually supplying what the other needs.

Anatomically we are not opposite. Males and females are just different versions of the same beginning. No opposition there.

Psychologically, males and females bring different qualities which, when we're open to the yin and yang of it, offer the full range of possibilities we humans are capable of experiencing.

Pregnancy and its related biological processes, including menstruation and lactation, are the only unqualified differences between men and women. But they are not in opposition, they are the female contribution to creating life.

Remember, according to Genesis, man *and* woman created He them. Not man against woman.

All of the opposition comes from the way we perceive each other.

When you shift your perspective from opposite to *other,* the foundational truth of your sexuality becomes apparent. You are not male or female in addition to something else. You are male or female first and foremost. Everything else follows from there. Once you open to the perception of the *other* sex or the *other* gender, you make room for relating cooperatively and complementarily through your specific gendered and personal differences. Doesn't that just make more sense?!

All the Ways You're Different

There are many forms of romance. Roses, champagne, silly cards, and making love in front of a winter fire are standard images we're all familiar with. They can all be quite wonderful! However, in and of themselves, these kinds of things aren't enough to keep the enchantment pulsing between you. Real and lasting romance is available only by appreciating and enjoying your differences.

We're going to describe a number of ways you can be different from one another, although our list is certainly not exhaustive. We've chosen to give examples from our own marriage to illustrate how all of these possibilities can exist in your relationship as well. If we'd used examples from different couples, one for each category, it might have appeared as though one couple had one specific difference, another couple another, and so forth. That is not the case.

Personal Differences

No matter how much you have in common, you aren't going to agree with each other on all the choices or match with all the behaviors that make up your everyday lives. You will have to learn about each other's ways and find creative solutions when you collide.

Judith: One of our funnier differences is how we use the top bedsheet. Jim likes it pulled up straight, just to his shoulders, and pulled out at the bottom. I like it folded over the blankets, all of it pulled up right to my chin, and tucked in tight at the bottom. We've laughed a lot figuring out how we could each be covered the way we like and still cuddle.

Jim: We have an entirely different relationship to dogs. I love them! Judith is a bit frightened of them and hates when they jump on her. She's learned to pause on any walk we take in order for me to pet and play with all the dogs we encounter. And I've learned to watch out for her, making sure dogs don't get too close, and then she can appreciate how much fun and how beautiful they are.

Complementary Differences

You have qualities that your spouse doesn't have and vice versa. Historically, men and women have discounted and belittled one another for not being as strong or as skilled in the same ways. How foolish. You can be even better matched when your complementary strengths and abilities provide support for what the other is missing and for the benefit of your relationship.

Jim: I hate bookkeeping and paying bills. I don't even like to balance my checkbook. Judith loves all that stuff, so she takes care of it. What a gift.

Judith: Jim loves cleaning up with the Dustbuster, ironing, and fixing whatever is broken. Not me! So I'm thrilled that he does it all.

Teach and Learn Together

Each of you has skills and interests the other wants to learn. It may be something concrete, like how to work the computer. It may be a point of view, like learning to go with the flow instead of trying to control everything. You can help each other expand your lives and enjoy alternating being the teacher and the student.

Judith: I grew up in Los Angeles and never really noticed the mountains that surround the city. Jim grew up in Detroit and hated how flat it was. When he came West he rejoiced in the beauty of the mountains. I learned from him to notice their different shapes, colors, shadows, and foliage. Now I'm often the one pointing out the gorgeous cloud formations, or how the mist makes a canyon look like a Japanese painting.

Jim: Judith has always been into healthy eating, taking supplements, and practicing disease prevention. In fact, I thought it was a bunch of hooey until some of her Chinese herbs reversed the onset of a pretty nasty flu. Since then I've learned more about food groups and I take supplements regularly.

Different Backgrounds

More and more often people fall in love and marry across cultural, religious, political, and other differences.

Judith: When I was a kid, my relatives lived quite a distance away so I was never close with any of them. I had only a few close friends and learned to enjoy being alone. Through Jim's influence I've become far more outgoing and social.

Jim: In Detroit, we counted over 125 relatives in my extended family and it seemed like most of them dropped by whenever they pleased. There was very little privacy. Because of Judith's influence, I've become more protective of my emotional boundaries and far more private than was ever permissible.

The Healing Power of Differences

Because you are different, you can shine the healing light of your love onto the distorted self-concepts and raw insecurities that plague your partner and he or she can do the same for you.

Jim: I grew up with a father who would actually say, as he pointed to his upper sleeve, "See this? I have three stripes. You have two. Don't ever forget it." I struggled with that to the detriment of my own sense of authority and impact in the world. Judith has lovingly encouraged the expression of my full power and has relentlessly pointed out my impact when I've been unaware of it or denied it.

Judith: I became a perfectionist in order to protect myself from my parents' controlling and hypercritical demands. Jim's easygoing, more accepting style has radically transformed my ideas of how and who I can be in the world—including making mistakes without pounding myself into the ground.

Each of You Gets Better Defined

Navigating and negotiating your differences requires you to articulate and define yourselves better. It's vital to open up and to explain why you do or don't want to have sex, go camping, believe in God, whatever.

Judith: At the beginning of our relationship, Jim loved to watch the television series *Cheers.* I hated the show. When he asked why, I couldn't really give him an answer. I had to watch it a couple of times with his question in mind to better understand my response.

Rather than finding the show funny, it pained me to see the characters make fun of one another, put each other down, and send the message that that was fun and funny. Jim got what he was looking for and he saw the show from a broadened point of view.

Jim: Last year we moved from Santa Monica, California, to the country in upstate New York. I discovered a love of

nature I'd not known before. Judith wanted to understand what I loved about dealing with the beaver dams
and rousting the groundhogs out from under the house.

I told her how I loved feeling in tune with the animals,
appreciating their right to live here too. At the same
time, I knew I had to find ways to honor my right to live
without those animals endangering our house and without my having to kill them. She said I became even more
attractive to her and influenced how she saw the deer and
even the mice she detested when they came to visit in our
kitchen drawers.

From Obedience to Maturity

Who you had to be to fit into your family of origin and who you
need to be to fulfill yourself in your partnership are bound to
collide. This conflict creates a healthy tension—healthy in that it
is to your benefit to face the need to become what your relationship requires of you and not what your original family expected
of you. You cannot remain the way you've always been and succeed at love.

But you can use the challenges of dealing with your spouse's
different ways to help you emotionally leave the home that required
you to be an obedient child (and may still to this day). Only as
an independent adult can you participate creatively and con-
structively in shaping your new family created not by birth but
by choice.

> *Jim:* There have been times I've had to support Judith by con-
> fronting her about how she was selling herself short—
> either in the world or in how she was relating with me.
> For example, she tended to be late, pushing herself to get
> "one last thing" done before we were due somewhere. I've
> continually reminded her how it's a disservice to herself

and to our relationship to keep me waiting and to pressure herself unnecessarily. Over time, she's become less compulsive and more at ease.

Judith: When we were first together, Jim became angry with me several times and really blew up. He behaved a lot like how my dad had been. Rather than just yell back, which I did with my father, I knew I had to stand up and refuse to allow this behavior. It wasn't easy. But acting like a responsible adult, instead of a victim or fellow "rager," made me much stronger and it made Jim aware that he couldn't just indulge his high volume at me.

Independent, Dependent, and Interdependent

In any marriage there is always the need for balance between being your own independent self and being part of a couple. There's a big difference between insisting that you can do your own thing; needing the other person to the point of not being able to function without his or her input and approval; and being secure in yourself, while at the same time being deeply connected in your marriage.

Judith: It's such a rich blend of life experience to remain independent—meditating alone by our pond, or cooking for company by myself, or having lunch with girlfriends—and at the same time have my life deeply intertwined with Jim's. It's the best of both worlds. The freedom to be alone or together makes it safe to be dependent, such as when I'm sick or feeling emotionally vulnerable and need him to care for me.

Jim: I need my alone time. For example, most days I enjoy an hour or so in the tub. I read, think, take notes, write out sketches for what I will develop later. Judith respects my alone time and my privacy. I also love being with her more than any other human I've ever known and wouldn't trade our time together for anything. That's the magic threesome of independence, dependence, and interdependence.

Sexual Differences

In the movies, it seems that every sexual couple hits it off right from the first romp in bed. Not so in reality. Very often sexual styles can be quite different.

Jim: I'd always prided myself on being a very gentle and tender lover. I wanted to please a woman as my first consideration. Judith experienced it as pressure to reach orgasm and told me so. At first I was stunned and hurt. After all, wasn't she my chief concern? Isn't that what a man was supposed to do? No, she told me, not if he leaves his own desire out of the equation. I had to admit, that's what I was doing and had always done.

Judith: I'd always prided myself on being a sexual partner. Jim was used to women who made themselves available to be serviced by him. I wanted both of us to be hungry and passionate, and our lovemaking to be mutual. But there had to be room for more than how I thought it should be. We had to consciously open ourselves to what has become an ongoing adventure in learning more about sexual expression and experience, bringing us so much closer.

Differences between Reality and Fantasy

We all enter romance with certain expectations of love and our lover. In the Third Passage we are invited to give up our fantasies in favor of the real thing.

Jim: I was used to a casual lifestyle. But when we started our company, The Magic of Differences, developing our workshops, promotional materials, mailing lists, and so on, Judith prodded me into working late into the evenings on weekdays (after I came home from working at the investment banking office) and on weekends. At first I didn't like it. Her let's-get-it-done, work, work, work attitude didn't fit what I had in mind. Still, I realized I was having more fun writing than going to the movies, more fun discussing creative ideas with Judith than watching football. My laid-back lifestyle began to recede and my life became far more meaningful.

Judith: I always imagined I'd marry someone who was pretty conventional and upper class. Instead, Jim came from the working class. I had to give up some of my expectations of social standing and refinement. But what I got in return is someone who is very funny, superintelligent, wonderfully adventurous, and always, always fascinating to be with.

Gender Differences

There are hard-wired differences between males and females that come with the equipment. As we grow beyond gender bashing, we can see that those differences round out how we live and love.

Judith: One aspect of male biology helps men keenly focus on one thing at a time, far better than women can. I see this over and over when something needs to be fixed. I would have given up long ago, while Jim patiently and with fascination finds his way to the solution. I know I can trust him to handle these kinds of things and it's a terrific relief.

Jim: One aspect of female biology makes women far better than males at multitasking. That's certainly true for Judith. She can be at her computer, in the middle of something important, as I walk into her office with a question. She'll look up, listen, answer, and go right back without having been distracted from what she is doing. Not me. If I am concentrating it feels like a huge disturbance to be interrupted. Judith knows that and is patient when she sees me involved. I cherish that about her.

Loved for All You Are

The richness of your differences plays itself out in the miracle of love in real life, a love based not so much on what you have in common but on how you share your unique selves with one another and how you negotiate the conflicts that are sure to come up.

In *The Magic of Differences* you must commit to a much deeper love—one that you will find only by enjoying and benefiting from being different from one another.

Exploring
The Magic of Differences

1. Review the differences described earlier. Go through them together, one at a time. Pay attention to how your differences are either easy-to-spot blessings—he is magnificent with the children when he comes home from work just when you need a break—or not-so-easy challenges—she loves the dog but insists that walking it is a man's responsibility. The first case is obviously not a problem. But how will you resolve the

dog issue so that both of you feel heard and respected? The challenges are perfect fodder for you—both of you—to expand and grow into more realized human beings, to say nothing of the intimacy that deepens as you treat each other with respectful attention.

2. How have you helped each other get beyond being emotionally stuck? In other words, how have you helped to heal each other's wounds?

   Discuss these gifts with one another, making sure to include your vulnerabilities, acknowledging your dependence, and appreciating your partner's strengths and insights that come from his or her different point of view. That way your differences become the deepest blessings of your being together. Commemorate them with "thank you" and "I appreciate you."

3. Take turns creating magical evenings and/or weekends designed just for each other. Consider the kinds of places, activities, food, beverages, sexual pleasures, and so on that would be exactly what your number-one playmate would love. Your own preferences are not the point during this experience. You generously and lovingly focus on what will please your spouse.

CHAPTER THIRTEEN

The Purpose:
Wisdom in Your Choice

*T*he primary way we learn anything is to be shown a perspective different from what we've known. Given the inescapable fact that your partner is not you, his or her perspective can open you to live and love in the fullness of who you really are. As you develop a deep and ongoing curiosity about yourself and about your partner, you come to feel more and more connected. In any moment, your curiosity can continue to reveal *The Magic of Differences* in your being together.

And what is that magic? First, you get to be loved for who you really are, and you love your partner in just the same way. Second, you get to experience the emotional freedom available only when you recognize and value the very real differences that make each of you who you are. And third, you never stop being enhanced and expanded by the process of co-creating your lives together.

There Is Wisdom in Your Choice

You didn't choose one another arbitrarily. One purpose of *The Magic of Differences* is to show you the wisdom in your choice of partners. With your soul's urging, you are attracted precisely to someone who pushes all your hottest buttons and also makes you feel wonderfully, marvelously special.

You get to see how your personalities and backgrounds are aligned in just the right ways to provoke and then lovingly heal your wounds. You enjoy supporting one another in this magical process and you reap the rewards of transformation that were unattainable without the other's presence in your life.

Brian and Lucy

In the first years of their marriage, Lucy was starved for attention. She was the tenth child of immigrant parents who had both worked hard to support the family. Lucy remembered being pretty much alone, when she wasn't having to fill in for her mother with the younger kids. Brian was a good kid, raised by an abusive, alcoholic mother and a passive, depressed father.

Lucy and Brian cherished being together in nature, enjoyed bowling, and liked the romance of dancing to old '60s records. They gave their Saturday afternoons to volunteering at a juvenile hall. They loved one another deeply and knew they belonged together.

But Lucy complained that when she was angry Brian shut down and wouldn't give her his attention. Brian objected to Lucy's yelling and withdrew when he felt he was being treated badly. She became progressively angrier. He protected himself by working harder to provide for the house they wanted to buy, which he thought would stop her complaining.

The pressure of the Second Passage pushed them into counseling with us. Their knowledge of each other didn't go deep enough to help them get past what they'd always done—push for attention on her part and withdraw from emotional demands on his—so they couldn't turn their caring into something that would support them both.

What they needed most was to stand their ground for the changes they had to have from one another. Lucy asked Brian to not shut down, especially when she was upset with him. Brian asked Lucy to appreciate how raw he felt in the face of her anger and to find a more loving way to challenge his remoteness. When he emotionally got it that she was not his raging mother, he could see how he'd projected his fears onto her in ways that were unwarranted. Through the process she came to understand that she often didn't receive his loving attentions and she needed to open up to what he was giving.

He realized he'd been reacting to her anger with the powerlessness he felt as a child. She was stuck in feeling the lack of attention that was so deep in her. He couldn't make an impact. She couldn't receive the attention she needed. They were a perfect fit!

Her outbursts at not getting attention reawakened the wounds from his abuse and pushed him to shut down, depriving her of exactly the attention she wanted. In order to respond respectfully and lovingly to her needs, he had to force himself out of hiding. His heartfelt request that she learn to be kinder and more receptive to his attentions forced her to open up beyond just being a complainer.

He had to leave the emotional home of his abusive mother and unprotective father and more actively take care of himself instead of disappearing emotionally. She had to leave the emotional home of her inattentive parents and become a person who could actually receive attention instead of only craving it. Their respect and understanding for each other's back stories supported the love they relied on to pull them through the challenge of their differences into the magic of new identities, new freedom, and new love.

They not only kept their love alive, but they also achieved a depth of real romance that was waiting for them at the heart of their sincere curiosity about one another and their willingness to change. By listening with respect to each other's needs, they were each invited to develop a new perspective and new emotional skills. That took them into a new world filled with love for who they could be, beyond where they came from.

Transformational Dialogue

At the heart of *The Magic of Differences* is the process of transformational dialogue—a genuine conversation in which a real verbal and emotional exchange takes place. It is a sharing in which you are so touched emotionally and intellectually by each other that you change your mind. What you thought, felt, and believed before is now different. You make yourselves known to one another and give serious consideration to each other's experience, establishing a basis in common, but seeing from differing points of view. That's what Brian and Lucy did.

In dialogue, when your positions conflict, you do not fall into dominance and submission where one or both of you wants his or her point of view to triumph, to be the only arbiter of reality. You respect that reality contains more than just what you see and know, and you cooperate in co-creating your shared understanding. That way each of you gets to be heard and valued while, at the same time, what you are building is a composite of each of your contributions. It is far more than just a superficial communication of information. It is a real connection and a deep communion. It is making love through conversation.

To keep love and romance alive, dialogue is fundamental.

Dialogue is open and unfettered—a flow of truth and personal meaning, back and forth, in and through both of you.

Through dialogue you learn to understand, respect, and value what each of you is bringing to your relationship, no matter how distorted and filled with old wounds it may be. It is a creative exchange that expands your emotional intelligence, your self-awareness, and your awareness of one another.

When it is successful, dialogue fosters transformation. Both of you are moved to become more open, compassionate, and emotionally alive than you were before the magic of your differences prompted you to change. You feel more connected, liberated to be even more available than before.

Compromise and Tolerate

It has been thought, in conducting a long-term relationship, that to compromise and to tolerate are the cornerstones of open-heartedness and compassion. But is this really the best we can do?

To *compromise,* as the dictionary defines it, is to settle differences by mutual concession. Certainly in situations where two people are entrenched, each determined to triumph over the other, for any movement to take place, compromise usually is the only method that will break the impasse. Both people are intent on struggling for power, each committed to the view that they have the whole truth. Because the other will not "see the light," and because they must continue living together, each one agrees to give up something he or she doesn't want to give up, as long as the other person does the same.

He gives up football on Monday nights and she gives up yoga on Saturdays. It's the only way they can see to stop fighting about how "foolish" they believe each other's interests are.

But neither one is truly satisfied, because both felt compelled to give up something they valued. Their compromise stopped the fight, but that compromise will maintain if not increase the tension between them, assuring that the impasse will rise again in some other form.

Intimacy is not about control and loss but about generosity and enrichment.

What about *tolerate*? When you tolerate something, as the dictionary makes clear, you endure it. You put up with it. The simplest way to make this point is to ask yourself, "Do I want to be tolerated?" We hope not, especially if you're being tolerated by someone who claims to love you. Lovers cannot tolerate each other without keeping their emotional and perhaps physical distance. To tolerate in this way is the antithesis of intimacy.

Complete Yourselves through Your Differences

It's often difficult to see ourselves without someone else's eyes. That's why it's crucial, for your emotional and spiritual evolution, to get your partner's help in waking you up to seeing yourself more accurately.

Since your soul is moving you toward wholeness, your partner's perspective provides sacred information in that he or she contributes to your spiritual development. But that doesn't mean your partner's behavior goes unquestioned.

Let's just say, for example, that your partner is bossy and that happens to be exactly what is required for you to learn to hold your ground. And holding your ground provides just what's needed to help your partner to give up being so controlling and self-centered. See how that works? It's such great magic!

Each time you are shown an *other* perspective, you get to exercise your capacity to consciously change your mind. Not in a trivial sense, like changing a shirt or making a different choice from the menu, but in a transformative sense. You have an opportunity to intentionally shape your life—both as an individual and as one-half of a couple. By seeing from a different point of view, your partner provides you with an *other* panorama, filled with distinct insights, attitudes, and ways of responding.

You can let go of what you bring that no longer works and take in what better helps you grow toward wholeness. You move beyond what was unconscious and automatic and become an active, discerning participant in your life together. Your differences create a powerful alchemy. You both become people you were not before, and you do so by choice.

Jamie and Carol

The Second Passage was particularly rough for Jamie and Carol, who had been together thirteen months. But they were committed to working things out.

Late one afternoon as they were getting everything ready for a dinner party at Carol's apartment, her coffee pot suddenly stopped working. Jamie said, with the flair of man-to-the-rescue, "I'll run home and get mine. It'll do just fine."

Thirty minutes later he arrived triumphant, holding a two-cup coffee pot for the ten people arriving later. Carol was shocked.

"Jamie, for God's sake, two cups?! What were you thinking?"

He was crestfallen. Here he thought he'd been the hero.

She started to cry. "This is horrible! Everything's ruined . . ." Her need for perfection overwhelmed her as she dissolved into weeping.

Even though he was hurt, Jamie put his arms around her and tried to soothe her.

"It's going to be okay. We'll do something."

"What?! What?!"

"I'll go and get another pot."

"We don't have time."

"Sure we do. And if a few people arrive before I get back, just tell them what happened. Life happens, you know."

"You don't understand . . ." Carol tried to protest.

"Look," Jamie stood his ground, "it's either me going, or you feeling miserable. You can choose."

"Don't be so damned rational."

"Do you have a better idea?"

Jamie left.

Alone, Carol had a chance to look at what she was doing. "Why doesn't he get upset," she wondered, "and why am I angry that he doesn't? He's out there getting us a coffee pot."

Carol had a choice. She could either continue to be angry, giving in to her distress, or she could give value to Jamie's point of view because she could clearly see it was a better response under the circumstances. In other words, she could remain the way she had been or, with the influence of his input, change her mind.

It's in all of the many moments like these that you have the opportunity to change your life. The issue may seem insignificant, but the opportunity is huge. Let go of the past and move into a larger future, or stay stuck.

When Jamie returned, a sixteen-cup urn in tow, he was beaming. Hero to the rescue.

Carol was in tears again, this time from gratitude. In a very real sense she had been redeemed. She had moved from panic and rage into an appreciation of how things could be different. She started to laugh and cry simultaneously.

"What?" Jamie was concerned.

"What a crackup I am. Ready to give up the ghost over a coffee pot."

"Let's be fair. It wasn't the pot. You really care about our guests having as good an evening as you can make for them, and I respect that. If it was up to me, they'd have had instant. But not you."

"Thanks," she whispered, "I appreciate that. But, you know, sometimes I'm a bit much."

"You can say that again."

For a moment she wasn't sure what he meant, until she could see he was teasing. Her tears gave way to full laughter. "But tomorrow," she pointed to his two-cup pot, "I need to know what you were thinking when you brought this little guy."

"You know what," Jamie grinned, "me too." They put on the coffee and listened as it began to percolate.

Theirs was sacred dialogue, filled with tender meaning, discovery, and deep intimacy.

For your own emotional and spiritual evolution, actively receive the help your partner provides in making you more aware of yourself. No one can spot your self-sabotage maneuvers as well as your lover can. Your partner's perception may not always be on point, but it is a deep act of love when he or she calls you on the ways you sell yourself short.

Jamie helped Carol to see that she was belittling herself with her version of perfection, and he helped her step into a self-esteem that better matched who she really was. He wasn't just a hero—he was a true ally.

From Freedom to Liberation

Many people are afraid to commit to one relationship. That accusation used to be leveled only at men. Now, as sex roles are changing, it's an equal-opportunity opportunity. There are so many potential lovers out there, so many sexual partners to experience, why settle down with just one?

The impulse to taste and sample is very human. Ideally, our adolescence and young adulthood are spent playing across the emotional surface with many different people. It is often a time of freedom and experience just for the sake of it.

Imagine a horizontal line with many, many points on it. Each point represents someone new. To move from person to person while dating has to do with being free. Nothing holds you in place, and that's as it should be. You are not ready to settle down. But your experience of intimacy remains limited because you aren't staying put, you aren't going very deep.

Then you meet someone special and you know in your heart you cannot continue to move along the horizontal line. That is what terrifies many people. All they can see is that if they commit, they will be fixed at one point. They will lose their freedom and be imprisoned in one spot with one person, unable to move.

If that is how you are looking at it, you have reason to be afraid. Who wants to be stuck? But there is another way to view it.

When you commit to a relationship, another line appears. A vertical line. By staying in one spot, you exchange surface for depth. You get to know and be known in all parts of yourself, through and through. Yes, the sense of freedom you felt along the horizontal plane passes, but in its place you experience liberation. You are progressively released from the constraints of your own fears and insecurities, your own unrealistic expectations and impossible dreams. You get to be loved for who you really are and therefore co-create a life that is deeply rewarding.

There is nothing wrong with moving along the horizontal plane if that's your choice. Some people want nothing more. But you make a tragic mistake if you assume that committing to a relationship will reduce what is available to you. A previously unknown and very rich treasure awaits you as you plumb the vertical dimension with its emotional and spiritual abundance. A long-term, deep, and marvelously fulfilling connection is yours. If that's what you want, your heartfelt and determined commitment is required. In fact, that is the only way to get it.

Maturing beyond Self-Centeredness

One of the biggest bugaboos blocking the growth of romance is the problem of the self-centeredness of one or both of you. Known as unhealthy narcissism, it is the inability to get beyond your own point of view. In common terms, it's experienced as "my way or the highway."

Narcissism, in itself, is not negative. We all need a good, solid sense of self in order to respect our personal and professional desires, ambitions, and the need for identity and emotional self-protection. But you can't experience a meaningful connection, let alone romance, if only your way and your demands are running the show. That's unhealthy narcissism. Then your relationship isn't mutually co-created but dominated by one-sided control.

One of the spiritual tasks of the Third Passage is to open your curiosity so that you can become more vividly aware of who it is *over there* that you claim to love.

In order to enjoy *The Magic of Differences* you have to hold two realities at the same time, your own and your lover's. There is no magic in a one-way experience. Only when you take each other's perspectives seriously—both of your needs, both of your personalities—can you truly be a loving couple.

It's like bread and jam. You can eat each alone, but the magic occurs when you combine them, neither losing their separate taste or texture but each enhanced by being joined with the other.

That's the beauty of The Third Passage—it purposefully requires your curiosity about each other to advance the spiritual awareness of your interconnectedness. To keep your romance alive, you must give way to love and allow it to help you grow up. You must let go of your childish narcissism and permit yourself to become an active co-producer of the couple that you are co-creating.

Moving More into Love

Once you get your loving, respectful attention over there onto the wonderful creature you are with, you are inspired by wanting to experience more and more of *The Magic of Differences.*

So you willingly learn more about disciplining yourself in the ways of love. You practice the spiritual basics of curiosity, kindness, generosity, and compassion. You do not want to inflict harm or neglect, even though it will happen from time to time. You can't always control your unconscious emotional baggage or know everything that will feel bad to your beloved.

When you move into the Third Passage, as best you can, you hold your lover's well-being as sacredly as you do your own, because the greatest purpose of *The Magic of Differences* is to propel you into a larger relationship with all of life—beginning first with the one dearest to you.

Exploring
The Magic of Differences

1. Curiosity is essential during the Third Passage. You want to be known and you want to know your partner. That cannot happen without both of you making the conscious choice to take an active interest in one another. What does that require? Asking! When you don't understand something, ask. When you want something, ask. But in so doing, keep in mind that your partner is not you and he or she may tell you something, or do something, that you don't expect. That's when the door to intimacy opens further. You are at the threshold of discovery. Don't withdraw. Ask, ask, ask!

2. If your curiosity is not returned, make it known you're really enjoying getting to know your partner more intimately and

you wonder why the curiosity is so one-sided. Here you're being curious again. Not demanding or attacking. Curious. When you get the answer, that's not a time to argue or debate. It is a time to explore. Ask again. Why does he or she feel that way? Be sure you let your partner know you are not interrogating but wanting a deeper understanding so the connection between you will continue to grow.

3. Kindness is one of the elements that creates a sense of romantic safety. But kindness is not automatic, no matter how advanced you consider yourself to be. In order not to lose sight of your love for one another, you must practice the discipline of kindness.

   The root of the word *discipline* is disciple, which means to be a learner. By fostering a discipline of kindness, you learn about each other through consciously caring.

   Make it a choice to do something kind for one another every day, especially when you are in difficult times. That's when your discipline will pay off best, assuring each other that your commitment is still there and your care has not collapsed. Then the future will find you even more closely connected because you were conscious enough to be kind.

CHAPTER FOURTEEN

The Problems:
Shadows from the Past

*S*ome of the most confusing problems you'll encounter are going to show up at the beginning of the Third Passage.

Why? Because it's scary to step into an awakening of self-worth and intimacy so rich that it makes you reexamine your life. The easiest thing to do is create a frenzy of fear and then retreat from the lovework that is beckoning.

Right about now you may be saying, "Aw, come off it. I don't have time for all this learning and growing. I've got kids, unpaid bills, and more hassles than I know what do with. I just want a nice relationship. Who ever said it had to be this complicated and demanding?!"

That's all just resistance and self-sabotage. Don't fall for it. Anything in life worth having is worth working for, and your love life is about to get better than you've ever known.

So surrender to the verbal loveplay that is the dialogue of *The Magic of Differences,* because a lifelong romantic relationship is the crown atop those things worth having!

Afraid to Speak

Shortly after their first child was born, Marianna and Jorge felt a change, a cool distance between them for which they were completely unprepared. To protect themselves, they each decided separately not to talk about it. To protect one another, each thought it best not to tell the other. Their sincerity and care sealed them into a double silence that fed a growing doubt.

"Didn't he want this baby?" Marianna fretted.

"What did I do wrong?" Jorge brooded.

Alberto, their healthy infant son, kicked and cooed and fussed and gazed at them, radiating the openness infants possess. His innocence bore into them, accentuating the guilt they each felt for the chasm of silence that had grown between them. But they kept their silence.

When he was six weeks old, Alberto developed a temperature that flared to one hundred four. Terrified, they rushed him to an emergency room where he was immediately taken for evaluation.

"Wait here," the doctor said, "I'll call for you as soon as I know what's going on." He was kind but firm.

They sat in a waiting room that was buzzing with the concern of many others, all whispering in anxious anticipation. Marianna and Jorge glanced back and forth. Each hoped the other would say something. Finally Jorge had to speak.

"I feel awful. Did I do something wrong?"

"Jorge," Marianna thought to comfort him, " kids get fevers like this. I only wish I knew more about . . ."

"No, no," he interrupted. "About us . . . you've been so quiet."

"Me? You're the one who's quiet."

"But you . . ."

Just then the doctor approached. "He has a virus. But he's strong. We're going to do a few more tests. If we don't find anything, we'll get his fever down and you can take him home. So why don't you two go have coffee."

Marianna found a corner table in the cafeteria while Jorge brought them coffee. She was crying softly.

Jorge swirled his black coffee, unable to look at her. "I'm so sorry for whatever I did."

"*You* did? No, Jorge, it was me."

"You?!"

"When Alberto was born I was filled with so much joy and love for him, but also for you, Jorge. For you. You are so tender, the way you feed him and carry him. The way you look at me. So much love. It frightened me. I don't know why, but I felt like it was too much, like there was something wrong. I tried not to feel it and I didn't want you to know."

Jorge smiled, wearily. "You and me, Marianna, we are the niños."

She looked at him, puzzled, her eyes red from tears.

"When I saw you nursing Alberto, I would walk away."

"Yes. I thought you didn't want the baby."

"No! I just didn't want you to see because, well, I felt sad."

"Sad?"

"And lonely. No, no, not about you, Marianna. My heart filled when I saw you and the baby, but then I felt sad and lonely. A lonely feeling that's been with me all of my life. I couldn't believe what was happening inside me. I felt guilty and confused because I should have been happy. I decided not to tell you. So . . ."

"I felt too much love . . ." She smiled.

". . . and I felt sad and lonely."

"And we both shut up about it." She was laughing softly. "Niños, Jorge. You are right, we are the niños."

You will sabotage your relationship if you won't allow yourself to be changed by love, if you hide from the power of love to transform you. That's what happens, you know. Not in every part of your being, but when you let love into your heart, you become someone new.

Think of it like a recipe. You take flour, water, salt, and butter, each a distinct ingredient, mix and bake, and you have pie crust. Crisp and delicious.

You take who you are, what you feel and believe, mix that with the ingredients of your partner's character and personality, heat with love and intimacy, and you have your relationship, unique and personal, a feast for a lifetime—your own living work of art.

As you saw with Marianna and Jorge, the pain of feeling authentic, soulful love can be threatening.

In our superficial understanding of love, we imagine only joy and sublime happiness. But love loves everything. It doesn't obey your fantasies of idealized romance. It seeks out all that has never been loved before. The clash between locked-up, frozen pain and loneliness and the heat of new love will hurt. It's just like with frostbite. If you immediately subject it to heat—it hurts!

People interpret the pain as evidence their relationship is bad or over, when that's furthest from the truth.

It's now, in the Third Passage, that love is the servant of your healing. Just as little Alberto suffered a fever to burn off the virus, Marianna and Jorge had to go through the fire of love's penetration to be healed from the pain of their past. She could not tolerate all the love she felt; it was "too much" and it scared her. And he had to face the loneliness he had always felt.

Love stripped them of their grownup facades and revealed the "niños" who had gone without the kind of whole-hearted love they now were feeling and creating with one another. Because they opened the dialogue, Marianna and Jorge could help one another live through the pain, let love cauterize the wounds, and emerge blessed by the magic of their love.

1+1 = More Than 2

You cannot be committed and single at the same time. Things are no longer as simple as they were when you lived alone or with your roommate(s). You can no longer manage your life as a sole and independent enterprise.

Jim: We'd been married about a year when I spent an evening with an artist acquaintance. He was a dark, moody man. Judith feared that he was potentially violent and was concerned for my safety. I had a sense of him that made me feel safe. I told Judith I would be home by eleven.

Our conversation was so rich that I lost track of time. At 11:45 I started home. I thought Judith would be asleep and I was hungry. I stopped at a drive-through for a cheeseburger and fries, looking forward to a picnic alone in front of the TV.

In the middle of a juicy bite, just settling into a documentary about cheetah, "The World's Fastest Cat," I heard the front door open and slam. Before I had a chance to get up, Judith came storming into the TV room.

"Where have you been?!" She was enraged.

I was startled and offended at having my picnic ruined.

"*Where* have you been?" she demanded.

"Me? Where have *you* been?"

"I've been looking for you, that's where!"

She'd been expecting me at eleven. As the time grew later and later, she panicked, thinking I might have been hurt.

I felt attacked and defensive. She said the artist was violent. I said he wasn't. Then we argued over what *could* have happened, which, given that nothing had, seemed pointless to me. We went on, back and forth, back and forth. Finally, at my limit of frustration, I shouted, "What do you want from me?!"

Judith stopped, looked me straight in the eyes, and said, "I want you to hold me in your consciousness the way I hold you in mine."

"Oh." She was right. I hadn't done that. Still combative, but with much less energy, I asked, "How? How do you want me to do that?"

"How about calling?"

"Oh. Yeah. Right. I could've easily done that." I'd been so caught up in my own world that what she might be thinking and feeling never came to mind.

I don't live alone anymore. Not only is there Judith and me in the flesh, but now there's also the Judith I keep in my awareness and the Jim she keeps in hers. That's how 1+1 is actually 4.

For your relationship to flourish, there has to be room for each of you. Always. *The Magic of Differences* is based on keeping each other in consciousness. Two realities to consider, not only when you're apart, but even in the middle of an ordinary everyday conversation. Two points of view to be recognized, valued, and given a voice.

Common Traps

Each passage has particular dangers that can interfere with or stop the flow of your progress through the full arc of love. These are what to look for in the Third Passage.

Analysis and Study

You may know people whose approach to love is the reverse of Marianna and Jorge's. Rather than opening to dialogue in earnest, rather than being truly present to be healed and changed by love, they intellectualize and study their process.

They are in and out of couples therapy, attend many, many relationship workshops, and read every book they can on love and intimacy and perpetually talk about them. But their relationship remains the same. They've become distracted, sidetracked from the main event by the *pursuit* of inner healing and relationship transformation, but unconsciously refuse to notice their unwillingness to change. They have the sense to know there is magic in their differences, that love is a powerful agent of ongoing redemption from old emotional wounds, but they're more entranced with analysis and study than with following their souls' loving push to actually be transformed.

Taking Things for Granted

When we love someone we want to do things for them. It's only natural. Out of that desire we may, however, take them for granted.

Tahnia and J. T. had been together for three years. When they came to see us, J. T. spoke first.

"She doesn't consider me. She'll do things like make dentist appointments for me without asking."

"But he always lets those things slide." She turned to him in self-defense, "You do! Admit it. You do."

"You're right."

"See?" she appealed to us, "So what am I supposed to do? And besides, I'm doing it for him."

We asked if she did other things for him.

"Sure. Lots. But so what? Then he doesn't have to even think about it."

Tahnia was proud of herself for noticing and responding to their differences and she was angry for not being appreciated.

Even though he was unappreciative of her caretaking, she was caught narcissistically, which can happen to any of us no matter how well developed we may be. As much as she felt caring, it was on her own terms. She didn't give him a chance to participate, and he felt invisible.

"Am I supposed to check with you about every little thing?" she protested. "That's crazy. I'd never be doing anything else."

We told her it was more about her intention. She'd been taking over as though he were still a little boy.

"Oh, that," she sighed, and sank into the couch. "Yeah, well, I guess I do see him as a boy, but only when he doesn't take care of himself." She turned to him. "I am thinking of you. Do you believe that?"

"I do. I know you care. Thank you. And sometimes I feel like a boy."

She was surprised and embarrassed by his public admission.

"Tahnia, this is therapy. It's okay if we cop to our stuff in here."

"I just thought ... well ... I don't know. Where I come from, you leave family stuff inside the family. Nobody knows."

Tahnia told us how she'd watched her mother take care of her father and vowed she would never do the same. "And yet, here I am, right where I said I'd never be."

"Look," J. T. said, "I don't like feeling like a boy and you don't want your man to be a boy. We're a good team." She didn't know what to do with his frankness. "So I'll make a public commitment, right here, right now, to take care of the kinds of things I've been leaving to you. Or I'll ask for your help. You can close the doors on your emergency rescue services. I don't want a mother. I want you as my wife."

"Are you serious?"

"Uh huh."

"Sure?"

"Sure."

She was grateful to be relieved of her "duty" and was glowing in response to J. T.'s desire for her as his wife. Their differences brought them to the threshold. With an open awareness, they stepped across.

Catering to Others

You're settling down with your relationship as your first priority. However, some of your friends may not understand the changes you are making. You may lose some of them because you aren't as available as you used to be. Others may feel jealous of what you have. Even your family may complain they don't see you as much, you're not the person they've always known.

This is a critical time for your future. It's the time when you are consciously grounding your relationship on the foundation of who you are, individually and together. You don't have to exclude anyone. You must, however, give preference to your life together to secure what you both want and need.

Some couples lose their way, not being able to claim the priority and privacy every intimate relationship must have. Or they betray love by falling back into loyalty to their parents and/or old friends.

When you expand the purpose of marriage or a committed relationship to include the emotional and spiritual growth of you and your partner, catering to others must take a backseat. Explain to your family and friends, with compassion and care, why you've become less available, why you've changed and will continue to change. Hopefully, that will help soothe hurt feelings and also enlarge their understanding of a truly intimate commitment.

Changing Sexual Desire

The ecstatic thrill of First Passage sex and the edgy even dangerous thrill of sex in the Second Passage are pretty much behind you. You are now an established, committed couple. There is no need for chase and conquer, for seduction and submission. You can't rely on being revved up by hormones or conflict. You cannot wait to be taken over and swept away.

Okay. So now what turns you on?

No one can give you that answer. Not because it's too personal in the sense of being private, but it's too personal because you and your spouse have to discover each other anew. If you are not prepared for this normal development, you may think things have flattened out. Not so!

Lackluster sex isn't a sexual problem. It's a problem of consciousness. It's an issue of not understanding that sex changes as your relationship changes.

Think of it as fine wine. The connoisseur is able to detect all the subtleties: the bouquet, the aftertaste, the area where the grape was grown, even the influence of the particular wood used for the cask to store the wine. For someone untutored, it's just a glass of red.

Your relationship ages just like wine.

In the growing intimacy, the details become flush and resonant. You appreciate each other's needs, wants, inhibitions, and embarrassments. Your more hidden and vulnerable aspects come to the surface.

As you stay open to the magic of the Third Passage, you and your partner enter into one of the most profound mysteries of this life—sex becomes more than just the physical act, it becomes an emotional dialogue between you, and your open and giving expression transforms it into sacred lovemaking.

Peaks and Valleys Level Off

As you become more in tune with and more accepting of one another, you will notice a leveling of emotional intensity. That's to be expected. You're becoming more aware of and nourished by the subtlety of your connection, the magic in the quiet still moments that are central to the romance you are building together.

Even so, some people succumb to the notion that if it isn't intense, something's wrong. They miss the high drama they see elsewhere. They may even pick fights to ramp up the emotional decibels.

Others want to go back to First Passage chase-and-conquer sex. They get exotic. Sex in the local park. In the bathroom at a friend's party. Anything to retrieve what once was. All of their attempts are manipulations, substitutes that lead nowhere.

Their desperation is understandable. What models do we have for successful, long-term, and still romantically sexual relationships? Where in the media do we see examples of vital, exciting couples whose marriages have been nurtured and refined through the joys and demands of their life together?

Yet there's no reason for desperation when you keep in mind that your love is becoming sweeter and richer. It doesn't need all those bells and whistles anymore. What it does need is *you*. *Your* honesty. *Your* courage. *Your* generosity. *Your* authenticity. *Your* trust in each other. *Your* willingness to receive love. *Your* determination to step beyond clichés and explore the adventure and mystery of your unique bond.

There is nothing wrong. You are maturing. That's not to say you won't ever have fireworks sex again, or fall into intense disagreements again, or hurt each other again. You will. But as you evolve together, an easy grace emerges. You see each other with finer and finer awareness. You appreciate each other for what is not obvious to those around you. The special connection. The silly play. The smooth cooperation. The soft kisses. Communication in a look or gesture. The ease with which you express what you think and feel. The curiosity to listen.

Your relationship becomes deeply personal, with meanings only the two of you share. You feel the power of your romantic bond in all the little daily moments that make being together so magical.

Exploring
The Magic of Differences

1. If you fear change, you don't need to do anything drastic to break through your fear. Commit to making small changes. Do something different every day. Drive to work a way you've never gone. Eat something you've never tasted. Approach the new person at work and ask them about what they do. Sit alone in silence for fifteen minutes, observing the thoughts and images in your mind. Take yoga, karate, art or photography, cooking, creative writing, something that will change you and make you more available for the adventure and mystery of love.

2. Make a list of everything you'd miss if you left your relationship. Don't leave out the little things: her special smile when you kiss her good morning, his great Sunday breakfasts just for two, the way she laughs at your jokes, his terrific foot massages. Whatever you can think of. How well do you receive and appreciate all that you've just written?

   Then make a list of how you've grown internally and expanded yourself in the world because of what you've learned from and with your partner. He taught you not to fear the computer. She taught you about antiques and the fun of junk shopping. He showed you the value of silence. She showed you how to caringly water the plants. Share your lists with one another. They will deepen your appreciation and your eagerness to do more for each other.

3. Opening up and learning about each other sexually can be very delicate. Fear, shame, awkwardness, anger, and unbridled passion can leave you emotionally naked. But for your love-making to continue to be fulfilling, you have to look beyond the techniques you brought to your relationship. They were learned with other people and may or may not apply.

   Take turns being the teacher in a hands-on sex class with your partner. Explore and reveal where you are most sensitive, what really feels the best. You may not actually know, so you will have to experiment. What do you need physically, verbally, emotionally? What kind of atmosphere do you want? Lights on or not? Music or not? There is always room for adventure. Your personal sex class can be terrific fun, really romantic, and extraordinarily intimate when you both give yourselves to learning and having fun together.

CHAPTER FIFTEEN

The Principles:
The Dance of Differences

*I*n the beginning, love is often confounded by magical think-ing—dreams of perfect, effortless, discomfort-free love. "I'll just *know* this is the one!" Then, when *The Clash of Differences* shows up, faith in the prospect of anything magical seems like a fairy-tale.

But in *The Magic of Differences* there *is* magic, and it's very real!

When you accept that differences between lovers are unavoid-able, and you open your awareness to the very real differences between the two of you, you can see that there truly is wisdom in your choice of one another. You love each other precisely because of and sometimes in spite of how you are different. And you know what a well-made match you are. That's good magic!

Principles of Magical Romance

You are not compelled to repeat a given action or reaction if it no longer serves you. Your mind, creativity, and will are extraor-dinarily powerful. You *can* change. All you need to do is practice the following principles of love every day, and the magic of life-long romance and intimacy will be yours.

The Other Person Is Not You

When you really get it that your beloved is not you, you can enjoy the wonderful range of differences playing out between you.

While we introduced this principle earlier, this is the heart of being loved for who you really are and the nucleus of the Third Passage, so it bears further development.

As soon as you grasp that your spouse is *not* you, you will have stepped beyond your self-absorption, which we are all susceptible to, and will have recognized your partner as someone quite unique. Then, when he or she believes or behaves differently than you would in the same circumstance, you can remind yourself that your way isn't the only way.

After Judith's brother, Terry, and his wife, Evey, had been married a few years, Evey said to Judith, "Well, I've just accepted that if we're going to a wedding and it's a friend of Terry's, and Terry is in charge of getting the gift, we'll be buying it on the way to the church. When I'm in charge, it will be purchased three weeks in advance.

"His way used to drive me crazy. I thought he was irresponsible. He thought I was rigidly compulsive. We'd fight about it. But once I was open and curious about how he did what he did, I could see it works out either way."

There really are many different responses to the same event—emotionally, intellectually, imaginatively, physically, and soulfully. Some puzzling, some funny, some bewildering, some affectionate. They will reveal the depth of your connection when you let go of believing your way is the *right* way.

All Relationships Are Co-Created Right from the Start

Again, it bears repeating that from the minute you met you began teaching each other what you'd receive and what you wouldn't, what you'd give and what you wouldn't, what you'd put up with and what you wouldn't, what you expected and what you didn't. You immediately began co-creating your relationship as equals. Not consciously, for the most part, but as equals nonetheless. Neither one of you was powerless. Neither one of you is powerless. You may be unaware of your power to influence each other, but that does not negate it.

Our dear friends Art Klein and Pat Feinman were both married when they first met. Their children went to the same school. Their youngest boys were best friends. After their marriages unraveled, and they realized they had an interest in one another beyond what they shared through their sons, they spent time getting to know one another as friends.

One afternoon Pat, who is an artist, gave Art a drawing she'd made. Two snakes sensuously intertwined. She used the drawing as her way of introducing the erotic into their relationship. Art was very impressed with her talent and her uninhibited generosity. He took the drawing as a gift from Pat revealing a deep sexual attraction to him.

You may be thinking, "Oh, pul-leeze, it was just two damn snakes. Don't get Freudian on me." For Art and Pat, it was a foretelling of their marriage. They rejoice in their erotic sensuality and it shows up in their successful work, designing and marketing lush three-dimensional tiles for their company, Functional Sculpture.

Your intimacy is always a work in progress. You have built your relationship to be exactly as it is. Nothing happened without either your active or passive consent. Anytime you feel stuck, even victimized, you can change it to better suit you. That is the power you possess. You have impact. Never forget that.

Curiosity Is Essential

When you are curious, you are eager to give your attention to one another. You have an interest and a willingness to learn. You are open and available to be changed by what you discover. You keep romance fresh and alive, because you are being recognized and valued for who you actually are. That's a real turn-on. An emotional aphrodisiac.

As you love each other for the persons you are continually becoming, the future opens to new possibilities and you are free to explore them. You can build a lifetime on that.

Our friends Paige and Don keep their romance alive and unfolding after twelve years of marriage and a nineteen-year age difference. For his sixty-fifth birthday, Paige gave Don a wonderful party. We all laughed and played children's games and Don was king for the day, complete with a crown, scepter, and a large bath towel that served as his royal cape. But her best gift to her husband was her ongoing curiosity about what turning sixty-five meant to him. They didn't shy away from topics like infirmity or death, and welcomed the freedom to understand one another at even deeper levels.

No matter how long you've been married or living with someone, there's no end to discovery. Your individual histories are a fertile ground of memories, impressions, and judgments that await exploration. Your current life will always provide new experiences to share. And the future is the playhouse of your imagination. What do you want it to look like? How do you see it unfolding? The romance of curiosity awaits you in every moment. Take it up. Take it in. Make it lush and giving.

Conflicts Fertilize Romance

Conflict is always a call for change. You feel constricted and upset and something has to give. The important word is *give*. When you hold the well-being of your relationship as your first concern, a conflict is an opportunity to give attention to something that needs loving care and compassion.

Judith: Every fight we've ever had, no matter the content, has been about Jim feeling unrecognized and my feeling mistreated.

Jim: Now, that's not to say there weren't very real issues to work out. We once fought over how I tipped in restaurants.

Judith: And how I responded to some typos in a business letter Jim sent, by unconsciously rolling my eyes in contempt.

Jim: But beyond the specific details, anytime I felt that Judith was being dismissive, it triggered a sore spot I brought from childhood and I felt that she wasn't listening to me.

Judith: And because of what I endured in my family, I was susceptible to feeling emotionally abused. If either one of our old wounds was touched, we'd fall into fighting.

Jim: Little by little, we recognized the pattern.

Judith: To heal those tender spots, we had to learn a great deal about each other's history. Doing that helped us understand our own vulnerability and what to do to treat each other with more compassion and care.

Jim: It deepened our intimacy, knowing and caring for each other even through—especially through—the hurts.

But what does that have to do with romance?

There is always an emotional distance at the center of a conflict. The connection between you is unsettled and may feel broken. Your partner may even seem more like an enemy.

To truly resolve a conflict so that both of you are satisfied, you have to push through together, sincerely respecting what is right about each of your positions. The caring and respectful recognition you give each other restores and reenergizes your connection, bringing you into the sense of oneness at the heart of romance.

Committed to moving from darkness into light, you are rewarded with a new depth of appreciation and a new measure of value for one another.

To get there, you have to have an *aha* moment, where you see the truth of your partner's feelings. That is an erotic experience, because you've discovered yet another level of attraction. Your partner is even more appealing, more fascinating, more magnetic, and your desire is even stronger.

You have to behold each other as equals—both determined, both contributing, both impassioned. Your admiration is the pulse of real romance. And you are proud to know you are emotionally mature. Neither one of you collapsed. Neither one wants to dominate. You care enough to insist that each of you as well as your relationship thrives. That is deep romance, one that lasts a lifetime.

Don't shy away from conflicts. They are invitations to broaden the ground of care and compassion you share, and when you say yes, they are a source of real and abiding romance.

Receive the Love You Are Given

Love can be right in front of you, but if you aren't in the habit of receiving it, then when someone is generous and loving you may feel that it just obligates you to do something caring in return. Or that they're just paying you back for some kindness you've bestowed on them. In either case, it's all about bartering and indebtedness rather than your open-hearted ability to receive.

The ability to fully receive love is not as common as you might think. At our workshops and trainings, when we ask, "Who has trouble receiving compliments?" the majority of both women and men raise their hands—without fail. And what is a sincere compliment? Nothing less than a moment of love.

If you have difficulty receiving love, you don't have a space inside to accept what is being given to you. You don't believe in yourself or value yourself or consider yourself lovable enough, so the internal feeling is how could anyone else? Then you reject the compliment and block the love because it doesn't make sense. It's not a match with your own experience of yourself.

We did a show for Wisdom Television about the difficulty of receiving love. Our guests, Jennifer and Brian, had been a couple for over a year and had just moved in together. They were engaged and planning their wedding.

Jennifer told us that whenever Brian complimented her, she would shrug her shoulders and "hrrmmph" at him. She was unconsciously throwing his expression of care and thoughtfulness out the window. He was frustrated and felt unrecognized, and said she was the world's worst at receiving compliments.

We helped Jennifer to see how she was teaching him not to bother. She realized that was her way to feel in control.

We had Brian pay Jennifer a sincere compliment. She tried to push it away. Although she was touched, she'd learned long before they ever met not to let it affect her.

They promised one another they would point out whenever the other was not receiving even the tiniest of compliments or expressions of love. Brian said, "It's like vitamins. We take them every day to stay healthy. I don't want our relationship to wither from emotional malnutrition."

To keep romance alive you must continually create it. When you cannot receive the attentions of your spouse, there's no way romance can take root and flower. No amount of boudoir photos, champagne, expensive jewelry, roses, sex, or wild getaway weekends can ever make up for the emptiness that blocks your receiving love.

The Spiritual Purpose for Your Being Together

As we've said, it's no accident that you've found one another. And you're not together just to have babies and pay the mortgage.

What is your long-range vision of being together? What are your joint goals? If you are unsure of the spiritual purpose of your relationship, simply look to where you feel the most unfinished, where self-expression has been most strangled. How is your partner well suited to helping you grow in just those areas?

We've written about how Bill, Jim's brother, and his wife, Kelly, met at our weekend training. Although they both were accomplished in their respective fields, they were quite dissatisfied with how they handled their finances. They also wanted to have a larger public impact.

Kelly had an eye for detail and a burning passion to change their life. Bill had a greater earning power and more outlets for developing income. They were allies in their commitment to root out and overcome anything that stood in the way of their expanded desire. They blended together like good magic.

They attended the classes and trainings they needed to realize their ambitions. They co-created a powerful weight-loss seminar and are co-writing a book to complement their presentations. They've launched a Web page (www.keepsmellinglikearose.com)

and continue to explore other possibilities. They look to each other for help whenever they are tempted by some distraction that takes them away from what they are trying to achieve.

They have become soul mates, well suited to maximize their individual wholeness and their growing presence in the world.

There is so much more going on between you than just the feelings of love and sexual desire. Your souls are engaged in a powerful dance of differences, hoping to lure you both into a much larger, far more meaningful life. When you know that, your trust and faith will be enhanced. You will take each other more seriously. You will laugh, play, and be sexual with more gusto, because you will sense larger energies in support of all that you are together. You will discover, again and again, the spiritual purpose of an intimate relationship—to bring you into wholeness through *The Magic of Differences.*

Exploring
The Magic of Differences

1. Ask each other a personally revealing question every day, whether it's when you wake up, when you sit down to dinner, or before you turn out the lights at night. You can even involve the children at dinner by letting them ask what they want to know about each of you. Then discuss what you learn about one another as a way to develop more curiosity and real romance.

   Make sure when your spouse answers your questions that you don't criticize the delivery or content. There's no "right" or "wrong" way to reveal oneself. Instead, focus on the vulnerability and trust that's being expressed between you, as well as on what you are learning about one another.

2. Don't let your lives just wander. That adds lots of unnecessary complications to being together. By staying aware that both of you count, you'll understand why it's important to sit down and figure out a life plan together.

    First, separately, make a list of all the areas in your life that remain frustrating or incomplete—wanting to be a better parent, wishing you had more time for leisure, looking forward to writing a novel, and so on. You could even include all the ways your relationship is out of balance—your wife hogs the playtime with the kids, your in-laws drop by without calling, your boyfriend won't propose marriage.

    Then answer these questions as they apply to each of you: Where do you ideally want to live? How much money do you want to be making jointly in five, ten, twenty years? Do you or do you not want to have children? If you do, how many? When? What do you want to do when the children are all in school or have left home?

    Then discuss the ways your differences can be put to use in helping each other change yourselves to create the future you each want individually and the relationship you want together.

    Do not let life just happen to you—it can only breed resentment as your unspoken plans and dreams fail to materialize. Figure out how to blend your dreams into a cohesive plan of action so you can actually have the magic of what you jointly want.

3. Make an agreement as partners that neither of you will let the other miss a loving gesture, like a pat on the butt for no reason or a midday phone call that says "just want to know how you are," or any compliments or I-love-you's. If one of you is too caught up to register and respond to the moment, the other will say, "Hey, this is romance. Don't let it get by."

CHAPTER SIXTEEN

The Payoff: Free to Be You

*W*hen you trust *The Magic of Differences* you are free, wholly free for the first time in your life, free to trust being all of who you really are.

Not that you've uncovered all there is to know. That adventure is ongoing.

But now you no longer have to hide your best and your worst for fear your lover will leave you, or laugh at you, or turn away from you.

You are free to be you and be loved for it. That's the payoff in the power of your differences, and it will make your life larger and fuller than ever before.

Everyday Life Becomes Romantic

Romance is no longer something you need to make up for a dreary life. You know romance waits in the simple chores you share, the little squeeze before going off to separate jobs, in the secret fears you reveal, in the silence of a long drive.

The Idea of Perfection

Your life seems perfect. But not in the old, static sense where perfection only meant something that is fixed and permanent. That view no longer holds up. You know that real-life moves and you move with it, evolving as you face your limitations and appreciating your particular development. And yet no matter how much you've changed, you are, in a very real sense, the same person you've always been from the time you were a child.

So what does perfection mean? It means *both* constancy *and* movement.

It's like setting out down an uncharted river. You know you are going to explore it. That remains the constant. But you can't know the particulars beforehand. They evolve as you go and are part of your changing experience.

However, because you've committed to creating your relationship *as you go along,* you now understand perfection as encompassing two dimensions. First, your continued, steadfast willingness to go forward. That is the stable underpinning that emerges from your commitment and it doesn't change.

And second, *as you go forward* you change. You have opened yourself to the flow of the unpredictable specifics you encounter as your life and relationship take you where they will. So movement and change are certain.

By emphasizing the idea of a passage—a crossing-through—you can have *both* the security and dependability of something stable *and* the zest and vitality of change and newness. You are liberated to experience *both* the fullness of the moment *and* the movement into the next. There is always a living, breathing current of openness animating your unwavering commitment.

Constancy and movement. Not one or the other. Both. Together. Perfection!

You can now be assured that your desire for perfection will not sabotage the flow of your love with controlling, unrealistic demands, but will move with it, filling every moment, every space, every thought, every hope, every everything to the brim, yielding a deep and sweet satisfaction. That is a mature and balanced sense of perfection, one that can support and inspire romance, discovery, and growth throughout your life together.

Your Differences Work for *You, Not* against *You*

During the Second Passage your differences seemed to be pushing you apart, now you realize they were enriching the soil of your future. They were catalysts for personal growth, creating an alchemical fire that burned off much of what might have stood in your way.

More and more you find that you can simultaneously live within two distinct realities—yours and his, hers and yours. You've grown past your self-centered need to dominate and you now want to live in a shared world with your lover rather than have your lover live in your world.

Your challenges are now opportunities to grow your intimacy even further. You still can't know beforehand how your challenges will benefit you. There is always the unknown. But you can trust one another to walk hand-in-hand into a future you will continually co-create.

Your differences provide the curriculum for your personal soul school. They bring you ecstasy and quandary. Love and fear. Ambition and conflict. Don't miss a thing. Want it all. Feel the depth and richness available when *The Magic of Differences* takes you into the heart of living love and down-to-earth romance as daily, practical spirituality.

You Need One Another

Because you haven't based your relationship on acting out sex-role stereotypes or trying to fit conventional expectations, you have had to invest in your distinctiveness as the stuff from which you've co-created your being together.

Whether it's the silly games and jokes and nicknames you've developed, or the raw pain you've shared when tragedy visited your life, no one else on the planet can play with you or grieve with you in just the same way. You have become closer friends, more trustworthy helpmates, and full equals.

Your relationship is a picture puzzle in progress. Some pieces you discover. Some you create. You know you need one another to keep the puzzle going and you cannot take each other for granted. That is the blessing of the new intimacy, when love and romance are based on the truth of who you really are. You can relax, trusting you will never be unimportant, because without you there can be no completion.

Conflicts Are No Longer Tragic

You now understand and respect that there will always be an area of emotional wilderness between you in which the wounds and baggage that have not been worked out still remain in the shadows. So you are bound to clash, hurt one another's feelings, disappoint, and misunderstand each other from time to time. That's natural and not a sign of failure. But now there are fewer crises, and nothing goes by unresolved.

We told you about our conflicts over Jim's short-sleeved shirts and Judith's baby talk. In order to work them out, we had to be willing to look at truths about ourselves that weren't terribly flattering.

Jim: I grew up hearing that the body was bad, sinful, the devil's temptation. One result was that I didn't like to shop for clothes. My objective was to get in and out of the store as effortlessly as possible so I didn't have to pay a lot of attention to my physical being. That was all unconscious and Judith helped me become aware of that.

Judith: When I began examining my baby talk, I realized I was afraid of being punished if I asked directly for what I wanted. That was a surprise and the opposite of who I thought I was.

Then we had to be open to change, moving toward a more mature self-awareness.

Jim: I suggested we go shopping together. I took seriously what I looked like and I paid close attention to what felt good about how the clothes fit, how the colors complemented my skin tone, and how I dressed my body. It turned out to be simple and fun. We both liked bold, solid colors, as well as an occasional striped pattern.

Judith: Jim helped me to see that I only approached him with baby talk when I thought he would be annoyed or would not want to do whatever it was I was asking for. I saw that I had to outgrow my fear and stand maturely behind my desires.

Through these early conflicts we promised to speak up and we expected to be taken seriously.

Judith: Dropping the baby talk didn't mean the child within me had to go. Just the fear. I still goof around like a kid, and Jim finds that very entertaining and very funny.

Jim: I've become keenly aware of what I like and what I don't, and have overcome the toxic belief that the body is to be rejected.

These are two very mundane, everyday conflicts that helped spur our individual development. As you can see, almost anything can be a catalyst in creating new ways of being together and keeping your romance alive.

Your Trust Is Strong

As you take each other in, you move more fully into the intimacy of your bond. You relax, knowing you can trust one another more and more as confidantes, playmates, sexual and lovework partners. You are increasingly free to drop your masks, the pretense and performances that have always protected you, so that love can dance between you, so that your *soulmatedness* can express itself more fully. You know, all too well, that your masks hinder the growth of your love, and you support one another, through active and conscious curiosity, to let them go.

You know you are choosing to commit to be together no matter what life brings your way. When you trust that there will always be magic in your differences, you can use whatever life has in store for you to learn and support one another. You are the best of friends, soul-bonded in your quest for deeper spiritual meaning. And together you are discovering the rich complexity that each of you brings to being a couple. With deep gratitude you trust the wealth of abundance that blesses your life.

You Cannot Fail

When you love with the truth of your differences as the organizing principle of your experience, you cannot fail.

Perhaps you just said, "Aw, come on, of course I'll fail if he won't marry me!"

Or, "You gotta believe it's a failure to me if she files for divorce."

We appreciate your fear and the heartbreak that's gone before. But you can fail only if you have your heart set on a particular outcome and that outcome never materializes. When you do that, you are not failing at love—you are failing at staying grounded in the reality of what is actually going on between you.

Or you can lose yourself in order to try to please someone, to win them over, to snare them into marrying you. That will be a failure because you must hide your real self to accomplish your goal. So you have no chance of being loved.

Either way, by demanding a particular outcome or by playing a game of pretense, should you "succeed," you've failed!

With spiritual generosity and integrity, you simply live your life, guided by the truth of who you are and the truth of the one you're with, and see what can or cannot be created.

When love is present, you show up as who you really are so that you stand separate and distinct, in the fullness of your individual lives. You know that for continued success there has to be two of you—two conscious equals, both aware of your contributions, both committed to the co-creation of your being together. When you keep that in mind, you cannot fail!

Exploring
The Magic of Differences

1. To stay in touch with who you are becoming, it's important that you take time to be alone, off by yourself. You need to regenerate, to explore your inner life without any restrictions or interruptions.

Read poetry. Take a walk or a nature hike. Work on your motorcycle. Weed the garden. Take a candlelit bubble bath just for one. Anything that lets you commune with you. This should be a restorative time, so no pressures, no expectations, no forced outcomes. Follow what your soul wants you to do.

Take the time you need to feel renewed and reinvigorated, even if it's only minutes during a hectic day. You will reinforce your sense of self and your relationship will be the better for it.

2. Choose to do projects together that tap your individual interests. You might want to do something major like redecorating part of your home. Agree at the outset that this will be a joint project with equal input. The end result will be, at least in part, something neither of you could have imagined alone. For you both to be satisfied, you will have to enter the unknown and open to your joint creativity. The result will look and feel like both of you, in different ways.

Or you could decide to visit five states in the next five years. If you have children, and if they are old enough, involve them. Rather than go on a packaged tour, plan your trips yourself. Make sure everyone has a task in the planning. You will be co-creating and teaching your children how to do it as well.

Perhaps these examples are too much for you. Well then, how about one Sunday a month, take the morning to tour a different part of your city, either on foot after you get there or by car, and have breakfast at a new place every time. Alternate who gets to choose the area and be the leader for the day. Or how about reading to each other every night before going to sleep and then talking about your different perspectives?

The point is to express your two differing interests, energies, and desires through a joint project that inspires you to develop yourselves and your liveliness even more. Then you are evoking new magic and strengthening your love all along the way.

3. Make time every day for both of you to talk privately about your day. Listen with curiosity. Express your excitement when good stuff happens for your spouse. Make a date to celebrate. Offer compassion and sympathy for the times that life has been difficult. Give your help, your comfort, and your care. Be kind. Be allies. Be best friends.

The Fourth Passage

The Grace of Deep Intimacy
Three Become as One

CHAPTER SEVENTEEN

The Passion:
A Foundation of Grace

In the beginning of love, you are gifted with *A Glimpse of What Is Possible* and you experience the promise of something altogether greater than you've ever known. That vision recedes, replaced with the testing ground of *The Clash of Differences* in the Second Passage. The clash gives way to the transformational dialogue of *The Magic of Differences* in the Third Passage, and now, by the Fourth Passage, *The Grace of Deep Intimacy,* you have learned to integrate one another's distinctiveness into the larger experience of your being together so that there is a grace in the oneness of your two different lives.

While terrible things can still happen to you and life can still present significant challenges, the everyday blessings of your co-created relationship help you transcend the impulse to victimize yourself by yearning and wishing for reality to be other than it is. Respect for reality is your anchor and you know, deep down, that is where the freedom to love fully resides. You appreciate the lessons of each experience. The trust you feel infuses every moment, whether you are facing discouragement or cuddled up watching TV.

Rather than the ephemeral rush of the First Passage, the joy you feel has become the foundation of everything you do. What was merely a glimpse has now been earned and grown into, a grace that is yours forever. It is at some times subtle and pervasive, at other times joyously ecstatic, and at all times secure.

Creating and sustaining love and romance is no longer a determined effort but the heartline of your life together. With the love you share as a safe, encompassing vessel, your intuition, your deep passion, and the sacred wonderment of your being together inspire you to more gratifying self-expression and even greater impact in the world.

Congratulations! You've arrived at *The Grace of Deep Intimacy.*

The Wonder of Being Human

There is so much more going on in this life than meets the eye. When you listen to your intuition, you feel it. When you notice the rich fabric of coincidence, you see it. When you love with all your heart, you embody it.

A Foundation of Grace

As you move into the Fourth Passage, what has been the experience of practical spirituality in your everyday relationship is transforming into a profoundly transcendent experience of grace.

Grace suggests Divine intercession, as in "by the grace of God," but it is grounded right here on earth.

Since the two of you have joined your lives so that you are open to one another, flexible and able to adjust, confident in each other's competence, accepting of what life delivers, you are no longer awkward or struggling but at ease. What you do proceeds from an internal wholeness you have built. You are not without your ups and downs, but you know you will continually be regenerated through your tested and trustworthy reliance upon one another. You are friends, lovers, and allies, welcoming of the world and giving to it. You are living in a state of down-to-earth grace, which then opens you to the grace that is transcendent.

Being aware of the nature of each of the four passages will allow you to know there is a quality of grace in each one that becomes more and more inclusive as your love matures. As you move along the arc of love, you will continually transcend your previous experience and be available to be graced by a love that is also Divine.

No, you don't drift away into delirium, leaving the world behind. Not at all. Rather, your day-to-day concerns become fertile opportunities to hold in awareness the reality of your own life as well as the real lives of those you relate with. You come from love rather than fear, and you want what is best for all involved.

The pleasure and satisfaction of taking the discernment and emotional creativity you've developed through *The Magic of Differences* into the larger world becomes an added dimension of your relationship, deepening the romance you share in your private life. In short, the more you love, the more of you there is to love.

Everyday Romance

You now know the quality of your life and your ongoing romance are what you make of them. As a reader of our email newsletter put it, "Anything and everything is romantic when my man and I share this warm, vibrant energy that radiates between us—from the most obvious, like star-gazing, to the most mundane, like flossing our teeth."

Your moments of sweet connection, shared humor, and overt affection can be experienced anywhere and everywhere.

With *The Grace of Deep Intimacy,* even a trip to the grocery store can be romantic. No longer beleaguered by "hating to shop" or "dreading the checkout lines," you give yourselves to enjoying the time together, relaxed and involved in choices you make and the chores you have to complete.

If the cashier is crabby, you no longer take it personally. Instead, you see a perfect opportunity to spread your love by asking compassionately if she's had a tough day or how much longer he has to work. You are engaged with life, even with strangers. No moment is too small to be a potential conduit for grace to enter the world.

You Can Trust Life

There are larger forces contributing to your life, so even when things seem to be going badly you know there is an underlying wisdom. You intuitively know that one direction is the right choice over another, even when it doesn't look so good on paper.

Judith: We had been living in a condo in Santa Monica, California, for nine years when a miracle occurred. It was Valentine's Day week 1999. We were in New York City to promote our first book, *The New Intimacy.* We made our second appearance on *The View,* and then, in a heartbeat, all of our other television and radio bookings were preempted.

Jim: The Clinton impeachment findings were to be announced the following day and that would dominate the airwaves. Certainly we were disappointed, and we had to decide what we'd do with four free days in New York.

Judith: How could we make the best of this seeming calamity?

Jim: The first day we browsed the art galleries in Soho and had a romantic lunch at a wonderful Italian restaurant.

Judith: Then we called our friends Art and Pat (remember the drawing of two snakes?). They lived in upstate New York in a little mountain town, population 436. Sure, they'd love to have us visit. So we hopped on the Amtrak.

Jim: They lived in a charming, 180-year-old, two-story farmhouse, complete with two dogs. There was snow on the ground. Everything was quite beautiful. The first day we took a walk, completely enchanted by snow on the pines, the birds and fluffy clouds overhead, and the crystal-blue sky framing it all.

Judith: We'd been looking to move out of Los Angeles for several years, but never found a location that thrilled us. Then we saw the sign. FOR SALE. Six acres with two streams, immediately adjacent to our friends' property.

Jim: By Los Angeles standards the price was a steal. So we made an offer and it was accepted. We planned to build.

Judith: Three weeks prior to our return trip to close the deal, another seeming tragedy occurred. I suddenly went blind in half of my right eye, due to a detached retina. I underwent surgery which eventually corrected the problem almost entirely. Still, the idea of living way out in the country now seemed frightening.

Jim: Before Judith's medical emergency, we'd made an appointment with a realtor to look for something cheap for us to live in while we built. Because we'd made the commitment to go, we went ahead despite Judith's fear. The realtor showed us three houses. Two were totally unacceptable. The third was nearly perfect—a 200-year-old farmhouse in great condition, on two acres with a large pond. We both felt as though the house said to us, "Buy me. I'm right for you."

Judith: It's in a ski town, regular population three thousand. The area caters to the out-of-town skiers, so it offers the doctor and the pharmacy I needed in order to feel comfortable.

Jim: We moved in April 15, 2000, and have never looked back.

Judith: The move made no sense on paper. With me being from Los Angeles, and Jim originally from Detroit, we've both always been city types. We travel a great deal and the closest airport is over an hour away and too small for non-stop flights to the West Coast. I had never lived in snow and Jim had vowed he never would again. All major shopping is over a half-hour or an hour away, depending on the store. And we don't ski, golf, hike, or play tennis—the four main forms of recreation in this area.

Jim: Yet both of us have never felt more at home.

Judith: And it all happened because of two events that seemed terrible at the time—getting preempted by coverage of the impeachment findings, and then my eye problem.

Jim: We trusted our joint intuition that the move was the right thing to do. It's been an extraordinary adventure, which we'll share with you in a future book. It's also been wonderfully romantic in so many ways.

Generosity of Spirit

As you pursue the truth of yourselves—individually and together—you will experience a freedom of expression that reveals itself creatively, romantically, and socially.

You are centered in the knowledge that no one should be mistreated, because deep down, each person is a soul crying out for love and recognition. You've developed a generosity that arises from the spiritual abundance you experience every day. Consequently, you take care not to add harm to someone who is wounded and in pain.

You are no longer afraid to speak up to strangers who make prejudiced comments. You know it's loving and respectful to confront friends whose self-sabotaging behaviors lessen who they can be. You recognize that you are a model for those who want the courage to stand up for more respectful, caring behavior. And you can trust your intuition to know when it is wise to intervene and when it will only make matters worse.

For example, imagine yourself in your local supermarket. You witness a mother slap her young son for being too rambunctious. What should you do? You may say something to calm the mother and to indicate compassion for the boy. "It's tough to shop when your son is such an eager and curious little guy, isn't it? But it hurts me to see you slap him like that. He's just being a boy."

Or you may choose to keep silent, sensing that if you intervene the boy may later be punished as a way for the mother to vent her humiliation. That would be a situation best left alone. Instead, you could express your concern by committing some of your time to work for better parent training in the schools. That way your upsetting experience would lead not to disempowered frustration but to grace-filled action, resulting in the most benefit for the most people.

Complementary Masculine/Feminine

Historically, it was thought that the two sexes were mutually exclusive, nothing in one resembling anything in the other. That belief has been the source of much abuse and violence between the genders, as well as agonizing heartache. It resulted in the misused phrase "the opposite sex."

The truth is each person is an outcome of the union of *both* the sperm and the egg. Each one of us is a mixture, in different proportions, of *both* androgens and estrogens, the male and female sex hormones. There is no such creature as a singularly and absolutely male person or a singularly and absolutely female person. We are all complex beings in which the characteristics of both sexes are expressed to different degrees.

We are not opposite but complementary. As lovers, men and women supply that which the other needs to heal and make them whole. Love is the medium through which they connect, explore, discover, grow, and come to as much fullness as is possible for them. We need each other, otherwise we live half-lives.

Another way of understanding this union is contained in the ideas of the inner masculine and inner feminine. These are not metaphors but tangible realities. The rugged man can be tender. The gentle woman can be fierce. Some men can be better caretakers for their children. Some women are far better at running corporations.

As you commit to the arc of love, the process calls forth that within you which is female if you are a man and that within you which is male if you are a woman. You are moved by the composite of the masculine and feminine you already are, toward a completion through the union with your spouse.

This idea is not new. Twenty-five hundred years ago, in his work entitled *The Symposium*, Plato told the story that, in the beginning, humans were both male and female simultaneously.

They were entirely round, made up of four arms, four feet, one head with two faces. They possessed great strength, power, and ambition, and they mounted an attack against the gods. From his throne atop Mount Olympus, Zeus, the chief of all the gods, ordered that humanity be punished. So, every human being was cut in two and separated. Since then, each human is born with the intense desire to find his or her other half.

There are many examples that illustrate the coming together of male and female into a balanced whole. One of the best is the dance.

Watching two talented and disciplined dancers move across the floor—whether it be the tango, a waltz, the flamenco, jazz, classical ballet—there is never any question which is male and which is female. Each has their contribution. The thrill we feel comes from what they are doing—joined, blended, separate yet together. We can see the depth of our gendered experience in its full flower. It is thrilling, passionate, uplifting, and ennobling.

The same dance is danced between two lovers who've moved along the arc of love and now express *The Grace of Deep Intimacy*. Being guided by love, they make love a reality every day, in the sense of being carried by love as well as expressing their love into the world. They are joined as soul mates.

Exploring
The Grace of Deep Intimacy

1. By expressing your care, you are putting forth a spiritual practice that can help heal the world. As a daily commitment, do at least one thing that benefits someone outside your family. It may be a simple favor. It may be something major like helping paint a neighbor's house. It may just be a

card of support or congratulations. You can do it individually or together. Then share the contribution you made with one another. This is a romantic way of expressing your gratitude for the fulfillment you feel together that allows you to give without needing anything in return.

2. Individually and as a team, begin conversations and/or projects that advance the future. For example, ask your dinner-party guests how each would want to see the world improved and how they would go about doing it if they had the power to do so. At a company meeting on team-building or leadership, suggest that the group practice their skills not just in the office but also in the outside world. Start a neighborhood improvement project with your neighbors.

    Share the generosity that is part of the fabric of your relationship with those around you. The key is your spiritual leadership, together—leadership that benefits us all and is an ongoing practice of grace.

3. Give a party for your next anniversary to honor all those people who have graced your life. Ordinarily an anniversary party would be focused on you. This time focus on all the people you'd like to thank for helping you become the individuals and the couple that you are. Create an invitation that makes it clear this is an event of grace and gratitude, and that the recipients are special not just because of family ties, or longevity of friendship, but because of their significant influence on your lives.

    If there are former teachers, coaches, Scout leaders, neighbors, religious leaders, or old friends who were helpful in your childhood and later development, try to locate them and include them.

If there are people who are deceased, try to include your memory of them in some way as well.

Besides giving thanks to all the people who have graced your lives, honor each person individually, or, if that is not feasible, give each person a letter detailing how he or she was significant in your individual lives or your life together.

The point is not to make this an expensive, lavish event, but to say grace.

Join together in your celebration of life's blessings and let grace speak. Celebrate all that contributed to bringing you to *The Grace of Deep Intimacy.*

CHAPTER EIGHTEEN

The Purpose:
An Aspect of the Miracle

*T*here is such a ripe spirit of change growing in the world. Increasingly, people are feeling the connection that binds us all together. We want an end to abuse and violence, hatred and war. We want an end to the high divorce rate and an end to losing kids in the process. We'd even like singles to find dating pleasant and enjoyable.

Now what could ending war and enjoying dating possibly have in common? You may be wondering why we've put these two in the same rescue operation. But, in fact, all of the things we say here that we'd like to see stopped or changed have the same thing at their core—they are all caused by the fear of differences. All of them.

Everything we see around us, everything in the human world, originates in the way men and women treat one another in their relationships and in their families. Men and women are the only building blocks of society. As we treat one another, so goes the world. Everything follows from that. Everything!

The Greater Purpose for Your Love

In February 2001, one of the most significant scientific break-throughs of all time was achieved—the mapping of the human genome. We now have a reasonably accurate picture of what it takes to create a human being, biologically speaking. But what does that have to do with differences and romance?

Well, one of the unexpected conclusions drawn from this new knowledge is that how an individual is raised may be far more powerful than the composition of his or her biology. We are definitely hard-wired, like the rest of the animal life on this planet, but what makes us human, what makes us distinct, is how we respond to the caretaking, or the lack of it, that we experience in our early years and beyond. Our responses form the foundation for what we think and believe, and who we know ourselves to be. But it doesn't start and stop with us.

How you were treated by your parents and other caretakers is a carryover from how each of them was treated by their parents. What they learned about love they passed on to you, mostly without ever being conscious about it. This idea goes back a long way.

The Bible says, "The sins of the father are visited upon the sons unto the seventh generation." Although not stated, the same holds true for the mother. And if it's seven, or three or five, let's not quibble. The family environment we grow up in has an impact far more profound than many people give it credit for.

You may be thinking, "Hey, people change, don't they? They grow out of their early conditioning." Of course. Many do. And that's why we're writing this book, to help you learn how to love beyond what you've known before. But think about *how* you change. You need the help of a mentor, teacher, therapist, lover, spouse, or an author—someone who can describe and demonstrate a new way of viewing things. So it always comes back to relationships.

Love, or the lack of it, is the basis of your relationship with life. When you've learned to be afraid of those who are different, life is a prison. But when you are guided by an awareness of discovering the magic of differences and you choose to live with respect and value for all of life, you not only reap the rewards of real romance with your special someone, but you also become messengers of love for all those you encounter. You can experience a sacred connection even with total strangers. You embody the transcendent possibilities you only glimpsed in the First Passage. That is the larger purpose of *The Grace of Deep Intimacy.*

But What about All the Pain?

Perhaps you're thinking, "This is really airy-fairy stuff! I respect people's differences but I still feel depressed sometimes. My husband's pretty good about feelings but he still can't forgive his mother for abusing him. I have a friend who's an advanced yoga teacher. She can't go out at night without her husband, because she was raped years ago and she's still bound up in her fears. She's ashamed about that. So what about all that pain, huh?"

Pain doesn't all disappear because you're in the Fourth Passage. One of the spiritual challenges in *The Grace of Deep Intimacy* is to develop an acceptance of life's pain. That will go a long way toward stopping you from suffering like a victim, without your having to deny the awful experiences that do occur. With an open-hearted awareness you can transform the pain from the horror it might have been originally and see it with new eyes.

In practice, this is what it can look like for you: You feel depressed. Your depression is pointing you to remember that earlier time in your life when you were made to feel bad about yourself, so you shut down and learned to act "appropriately." In other words, you had to de-press yourself in order to fit in, to be acceptable, even to survive. Rather than assuming that's just the way things are and continuing to succumb to the depression, you can use it as an impetus to push yourself out of your shell and discover that most people don't behave toward you the way your family did. It may not be easy, but you no longer have to be loyal to where you came from by keeping yourself down.

In order for your husband to stay angry at his mother for her abuse, he must still live as though he is under her thumb. That just keeps him her little boy. But now he can look back, without exonerating her, and see that she too was abused as a child and didn't know any better. He can see that she never let go of her rage. By abusing him, she transferred it onto him and if he doesn't let go of his anger, he'll do the same. He won't just be her boy, he will be *her*. He must work to develop his compassionate wisdom. He may have to stay away from her if she's still raging, but he no longer has to live in the past as if it's real today.

Your friend who was raped may want to volunteer at a rape counseling center. She can face her fear, indirectly at first, and fortify herself through helping others. Her sense of shame will also diminish as she does the lovework of truly receiving her husband's full acceptance of who she is. As long as she feels shame, she can't completely appreciate his loving and respectful attention to her needs.

By expanding your point of view, by seeing things differently, your pain can be transformed. You don't deny it. You integrate it into your sense of self, you use it to understand the next step in your evolving humanity, and you change your relationship with all of life.

The Sacred in the Mundane

We've said that the sacred is that which is not immediately apparent and yet capable of inspiring awe and reverence. It draws your attention by energizing your respect and love. But, again, it is not immediately obvious to the senses.

When you look at a piece of art, the surface is beautiful in the way the colors are blended and set off to create the shapes on the canvas and render the artist's message. Yet there is more. As you take it in, the entire piece can transport your imagination into that realm of expanded experience you can't put words around. But you know it's there. You know it's real. You can feel it, sense it, intuit it, and, in some instances of breakthrough, you can "see" a deeper meaning directly.

When the sacred is present in your relationship, that same sense or feeling is present, inspiring your response to an ever-changing and deepening admiration and love.

There is always movement. Life and love are a constantly unfolding process. You know that from all you've gone through together, including the subtle ebb and flow of feelings and thoughts as you interact with your beloved.

You contain two realities. One is inexpressible but you know it is real. It has been called the breath of life, the numinous, élan vital, the holy. The other is perceptible. You can see it, feel, touch, taste, and hear it.

You hold your spouse in your consciousness, and you lead your life with both of you in mind. The joy of doing so is no burden. Quite the contrary, it is a sweet liberation.

As you are moved by *The Grace of Deep Intimacy,* the everyday world becomes more alive. Not that there is necessarily more action, but you are drawn by the miracle of sheer existence. That you are, that your beloved is, that life buzzes and throbs around you, excites a sense of reverence. Nothing short of deep appreciation is enough. You are an aspect of the miracle, embedded at the heart of it. Every moment holds the promise of carrying you beyond concrete reality into the awesome sense of what you and we are all part of. The mundane radiates the sacred and the sacred gives meaning to the mundane. It is everywhere all of the time.

Doorway to Oneness

More and more people are seeking spiritual meaning in their everyday relationships, something more soulful in their lives. By the time you reach the Fourth Passage you are an embodiment of a spiritual, soulful life. You have grown into an awareness that is inclusive not just of those nearest you but is all-encompassing. You appreciate the extent to which you are an active participant in the shaping of your life. You are respectful of how life brings you what you need to learn. You experience that through a sense of oneness with each other and in your connection to all of life. And you are liberated from narcissistic loneliness as you realize that your actions never take place in isolation. You are always, always affecting the life around you as it affects you in turn.

The Grace of Deep Intimacy emerges as you extend beyond your love for your spouse, largely achieved during *The Magic of Differences,* to experience a transcendent love for all people. That's not to say you approve of everything. Not at all. It simply means you can see yourself in others, thereby never again alienating your vision, your heart, or your being on this earth.

Judith: In 1985 I had a foretelling of the truth of connectedness when I went to the Soviet Union on a psychiatric study tour. We were in the southern regions of Kazakhstan and Tashkent. At an outdoor market I saw a very old, dark-skinned Muslim man with a deeply sun-withered face, crouching against an outside wall. His two front teeth were gold and they reflected the light of the sun. I was repulsed—by his age and his teeth.

But then, just as quickly and not by deliberate choice, I felt my soul say, "Look again. He is you." In that moment the man became extraordinarily beautiful. He hadn't changed. He was perfect just exactly as he was. And I knew that within me there was also an old person, a male person, someone who could have gold teeth.

I am grateful to that man. He was my partner in a shift of vision and consciousness, a glimpse of my spiritual self through his distinctive presence. I was no longer alienated. I was him. He was me. We were connected. Soul to soul.

My eyes welled up with tears of gratitude and awe for the down-to-earth spiritual expansion of my perception. I was touched by my soul teaching me to see with larger eyes so that I could relate within a wider circle of connection.

That is one of the most profound purposes of *The Grace of Deep Intimacy*—to show you that this wider vision can be yours when you move beyond your prejudgments, your prejudice against differences.

Ego and Humility

When you first surrender into the arc of love, you are like carbon buried in the earth before heat and pressure turn it into a precious diamond. Being spiritually young, you can be caught up in your own ego. Ego is that sense of self made up of the judgments, decisions, appraisals, and conclusions you've arrived at as you responded to the world around you. It is the world of your personal past and the patterns you established by which to live in that specific and particular world. When you are unaware of the content of your ego, it functions as the dictator of the way things *should* be.

We don't condemn the ego. Without it you could not function in this life. But being wrapped up in it leaves you ignorant of the needs and ways of others, and there's no room for a real and meaningful connection.

Fortunately, your desire to be loved prompts you to move beyond your naive narcissism to discover the joys of being with others—as they truly are. And, of course, you get to be who you really are. You get to change and grow and savor the very real grace of your unfolding awareness.

In the Fourth Passage your soul takes over more and more, relegating ego to the status of a memory bank, not the director of your experience. You even enjoy healthy narcissism as you feel free to claim greater self-expression, creativity, and a larger presence in the world. You experience your excellence as an endowment from a Larger Reality, to be shared for the benefit of all.

As our friend Joel Roberts says, "Humility is not the denial of your gifts. Humility is acknowledging the Source of your gifts, then giving them fully."

To keep romance alive, you must continually free yourself from the fear, shyness, and false humility that block the full expression of your love. Romance thrives in the rich soil of new expression, new freedom, new life.

Blessed with *The Grace of Deep Intimacy,* you are at home inside yourself, available for so much that was previously denied, inhibited, and locked away behind control, proper form, stifled imagination, and much, much more. You are now capable of being romantic whenever you desire, because you know, with all true humility, that real romance arises from your simply being the wondrous, always-changing gift of life that you are.

Synchronicity Confirms Your Larger Connection

The stronger your spiritual connection, the more you'll experience life events being magically in sync. You will see your inner life reflected in the outer world. For those of you new to this experience, it's called "synchronicity."

Remember Erin meeting Anders immediately after the drunken woman in the ladies' room told her she was about to meet the most important person in her life? Had it been just any man, it could have been the power of suggestion. But it was Anders, the man she'd wanted to meet years before. That's synchronicity!

Judith: A few years after we were married, Jim and I took a one-week road trip through Arizona and New Mexico. On the way home we started roughing out the script for our *Breaking through Resistance* self-help audiotape. We disagreed about a key point and our exchange became very intense. You could call it overheated!

Jim: Just then, I looked at the dashboard and blurted, "Judith, look at the heat gauge. The car's burning up!" The gauge was in the red, where it hadn't been at any time before. Concerned that something was wrong, we pulled into the next gas station and had it checked. "Nothing's wrong here," the mechanic said.

Judith: Relieved, we got back on the road, the gauge back to normal. A few miles later, our argument flamed again. And the heat gauge was back in the red again. We laughed and laughed, and the tension broke. At no time during the rest of the trip did the gauge act up. Nor did we.

Jim: Our anger was reflected back at us, telling us to stop our own resistance and cool off! We did, and it's one of the best examples of synchronicity we've experienced.

Synchronicities nourish your spirit and keep you open to the greater mystery of the life you share with one another. And if that ain't romantic, we don't know what is.

Your Love Is a Model for Others

You are now showing others the way, whether you are aware of it or not. Your relationship stands apart from those just getting by, just tolerating one another. And people watch to see how you do it, what it is that makes your love shine. They may even ask your secret, you're so obviously still in love with each other.

And you might tell them, as a couple in their seventies told us after attending our presentation at a Whole Life Expo in Pasadena, "We love each other more now than in the beginning because there's so much more to love. And we love that we're so different from each other. That keeps it exciting and fascinating all the time."

You may take younger or newer couples under your wing and counsel them in the ways you've learned to keep romance alive, to solve conflicts as a team of truth-seekers, to know that self-centered control spells failure every time. And you can be sure that your children are learning from you, absorbing your consciousness, and watching as you change with each other. They will take this into their dating and into their marriages, and you will be there as a lovely, gentle influence for their success.

Exploring
The Grace of Deep Intimacy

1. Take the lead and invite friends over for a couples' evening once a week or once a month. Make it casual, maybe a potluck

dinner or just dessert. Make it clear in your invitation that your goal for the evening is to create a safe space for everyone to discuss how they can use their relationships to better serve the community, to serve as better models for their kids, to better express their own potential as individuals and as a team.

You can take turns as couples moderating the discussion. But it will be your responsibility to use your knowledge of *The Magic of Differences* and the four passages, as well as your own experience together, to help provide a safe, respectful, and fun space for your group to talk about and learn from their fears, desires, and challenges. Make sure you share your own issues and discoveries. You will be exercising your leadership as lovers and helping create a more loving consciousness in the world.

2. Start an ongoing love letter that goes back and forth between the two of you. You might write only a sentence or two before you pass it to your spouse or you might write several paragraphs. You may want to write in email or on paper. You may keep each one separate or make it a running dialogue.

Just to make it more fun, if you write on paper you may want to hide your love letters in places your beloved will discover by surprise. Make sure you explore all types of loving expressions, from torrid to zany, sentimental to forthright. Let your hearts' fullness grace each page as you make love to one another through the words of your souls' celebration.

3. No matter where along the arc of love you are, you cannot eliminate pain from your life. But, as we said, you can accept and integrate the hard times, offering compassion and support to one another, and reaping the lessons they contain.

One strategy for doing that is to say to yourself and each other, "The story isn't over yet. Let's stay focused on what is happening now and wait to see the outcome." That way you don't hold back and you don't flee. You respect life by dealing with it on its terms as well as your own. Then you can share in the mystery as it unfolds and moves you along on your path.

Sometimes that can be very difficult when someone you love is dying or your child is in trouble. But even in the dark hours, romance is present in your support for one another and your deep, deep gratitude for going through it together.

Remember—"The story isn't over yet. Let's stay focused on what is happening now and wait to see the outcome."

CHAPTER NINETEEN

The Problems:
Forgetting You Are Human

It may seem like there couldn't possibly be any problems when you reach the spiritual awareness of the Fourth Passage. After all, you've been through so much together, and it's only fair that you finally get to be on automatic pilot and just coast, right? You're evolved. You've demonstrated you're responsible. So what could cause problems?

Well, we're always human. Always! While we are in this life, we are a mix of the mundane and the transcendent. We're part angel, part animal, part conscious, part unconscious, carrying a vision that looks out and beyond while we are embedded in the clay of this experience. We know what we know and we know there is so much more we don't know. We are bold and fearful, sophisticated and naive, filled with courage and painfully vulnerable.

All of this means we are capable of expressing the heights of brilliance as well as moments of confounding ineptitude. While there are fewer problems as we mature in love, we can always step on our own laces and fall flat on our own sense of self-importance. That's true as long as we're alive. So here are a few things to watch out for.

Your World Has Changed

You've changed and your world has changed as well. For some people that can be a lot more than they expected.

Things Were Supposed to Get Easier

A number of years ago we had lunch with an entrepreneur in the television business. At the time he was working with the government of the Soviet Union to set up better communication facilities in Moscow and outlying regions. He was very well-respected and very successful.

We were talking about what had surprised us most in life. He said he'd always thought that the older you got the easier life would be, and was very disappointed to find that wasn't the case. "The older I get, the more skilled and aware, the more complex projects and responsibilities I take on, and they're always a challenge because they come with lots of problems." We all laughed in knowing agreement.

Spiritual evolution does not mean the end of responsibility, but responsibilities are no longer a burden. They are simply, as it's been defined, the ability to respond. They are the means by which we express the mastery we've been developing.

Still, there is in all of us that deep-down wish to be taken care of, to have an effortless life. It's an echo of the Garden of Eden. Perhaps that comes after we pass on. But as long as we are alive, responsibility is part and parcel of living, part of being on this earth.

The Outer World Holds Less Pull

Because love, joy, pleasure, and spiritual meaning now play more ardently in your relationship, the outer world may seem less appealing. The glitter is less compelling. The turmoil is more disheartening. You are drawn inward, both individually and within the soul-mated vessel you've co-created. More frequently than ever, you may need a break, a time to let go of worldly demands, to relax and regenerate. If interest and money allow, you may even be drawn to take a spiritual minisabbatical, studying and/or healing at an ashram, a spa, a learning institute of some kind, or even a cabin in the woods.

There is the idea that the goal of spirituality is to resign from human life. But if you reject this world entirely, that can be very harmful. After all, many of those we call saints and enlightened ones don't resign. They live life differently, placing themselves directly in the hurly-burly of being human and offering their wisdom to those who are interested. They accept the demands and take breaks and vacations when necessary.

There are others who believe human passion is antispiritual. They withdraw by suppressing what they feel. But when you look at the people we most revere, they didn't renounce the world. They worked *in* the world. They were passionate, outspoken, interested in ideas as well as in fundrasing, much like Mother Theresa and Martin Luther King.

The Creator has given you talents and desires. *The Grace of Deep Intimacy* is a call to express them—for the benefit of your wholeness and for the betterment of the world.

Some Changes May No Longer Be Optional

You may have been going along dreading work on Mondays, or telling yourself you'll lose the weight someday, or hoping to go back to school when the inheritance comes in. But until now you never felt you had to make the change.

Now, as the grace of your spouse's full love and support blesses your life, you find that these things you've tucked into the shadows of awareness can no longer be ignored. It is no longer enough to put up with just tolerating your work, living in a body you don't like, or depriving yourself of the education you've always wanted.

While your determination to have what you want is exciting and truly empowering, just remember that life is still life and getting what you want won't be hassle-free. While love has provided a solid base that supports your ambitions, you'll have to manage any disruptions to your lifestyle, finances, family, and friends. But that's no reason to stop yourself. It's just grace clearing the way for you to experience more of who you are.

Healing Old Wounds

During the Fourth Passage, conflicts still arise. They may not be so loud and contentious, but they can trigger even deeper, even more psychologically primitive wounds, some that may have occurred before you were even able to speak. Incidents buried beneath layers of self-protection. Judgments you made about yourself before you could clearly discriminate. It can come as an alarming surprise. Why does this happen? Because, when love is present, all that has never been loved before can come to the surface, because it must and because it can.

Here's how it works. You're a little person, say before the age of two. Something has happened that terrified you but you had no way of releasing the charge. It all happened before you had words with which to organize it and hold it in memory. So it buried itself in your body. But it happened and it's still with you, though unconscious.

When your relationship is anchored in trust, and you are freer with your partner than you've ever been with anyone, a conflict can dislodge that old dormant terror and it rushes to the surface. It seems like all hell has broken loose and you feel way out of control. But you have enough presence of mind not to want to hurt your partner or retreat from the struggle. You know it's old baggage and not your spouse's fault that you are feeling so terrible. Nevertheless, you are flooded with undercurrents of the old hurt and fear. And it's the love between you that has made it safe for the old wound to surface so it can be healed.

We worked with a couple who were in a pitched battle because, after a wonderful silver anniversary trip to Europe and a big party given by their children, he was suddenly upset by the way she kept house. Never caring much about it before, now he would launch into a rage when, from his perspective, even the slightest thing was out of place. "I just like my home to be orderly," he defended. "Is that too much to ask?"

The incident that brought them to us had to do with, of all things, the toaster. She had left it out that morning. "It belongs in a bottom cabinet near the sink," he said. They had been together long enough, enjoying an otherwise rich life together, to know there was more going on than just the toaster.

As it turned out, his mother had started drinking just after he was born. Her mood swings had been severe and she could sometimes be very mean. She had pulled herself together with the help of a therapist when he was almost four and she never drank again. But no one ever talked about it, so he had no idea about what had happened.

After gently probing him about the way his childhood home was kept, a muted memory washed over him and he began to weep. To be certain it wasn't just a fantasy, or an image he'd invented to make sense of what he suspected, he later called his mother to talk about what the family had been like when he was little. She confessed her drinking problem. It had been a burden of guilt for her and she was grateful to finally release it. She described how she was frightened of being a mother and how she demanded that everything, including her little boy, be perfect so she could feel secure.

Although he had no tangible memories, his feelings made sense given what she'd told him. His desperate need to keep the house in order had arisen because his long-buried terror of being imperfect had been touched by all of the loving attention he'd received during their anniversary celebrations. Once he understood, he relaxed. "I don't want it to be a mess," he smiled, "but it doesn't have to be white-glove perfect." An old, buried wound had surfaced to be recognized, accepted, and let go.

When conflict occurs and it goes in a direction that doesn't make sense, please don't make the mistake of thinking there's something wrong with your relationship, or something wrong with you. That would be far from the truth. You have just hit a psychic payload and it's time to dig up the treasure.

Ego Distortions

Just as no one is happy all the time, no one is in a state of grace all the time. So there are problems that can arise from the pitfalls of narcissism, such as misconceptions and misinterpretations, or from insecurity, ambition, or any of the other vulnerabilities we humans grapple with. Even though you have become quite centered and self-confident through the transformational process of the arc of love, you can never be entirely free from being snagged.

Spiritual Greed

You love the freedom and expansive connection you feel when you're in a state of grace, but rather than feeling grateful for those periods of effortless and awesome intimacy, and accepting life even when you don't feel so blessed, you find yourself yearning, maybe even demanding, to feel grace all of the time. That is spiritual greed.

When you are feeling insecure you may even pray to recapture that feeling. You may try to make a deal with God—"I'll do this if you give me that." Or you may try to purify yourself, believing purity will open the way to continuous grace.

We've worked with any number of people who believed that spirituality meant only feeling good. Only feeling love. Never feeling angry or disconnected or worried. They wanted to be "fixed" so they could perpetually feel love and kindness.

It denies the fullness of life. It rejects an entire dimension of living. You refuse creation as the Creator created it and you reject the light-and-shadow complexity of love's perfection. You end up with a false sense of love, because spiritual greed closes out the full spectrum of reality and replaces it with an impossible fantasy.

If you notice impulses in this direction, remind yourself that you are not the Source. You are an exquisite channel through which the Source expresses itself when you are open, heart-filled, and connected to all of life. Remember that one of the best ways to stay open is through the deep, intimate connection you share with the one you love.

Spiritual Arrogance

All people do not aspire to the same level of self-knowledge and self-development. Neither do they have the same goals for their romantic relationships. There are definite differences between the levels of consciousness and the depth of love any two couples experience. The truth is, all people are not created the same. Even if, like you, they seek deep grace, they may not be capable of what is required of them.

Since you can't avoid observing the distinctions between your relationship and those of your family and friends, you can lapse into feeling superior. That is spiritual arrogance.

While we're not all the same, we are equals in that each one of us can live the fullness of our existence, the fullness of engaging in the joys and challenges of living and loving. To avoid spiritual arrogance, keep in mind that different couples can be full without having the same range of possibilities. There's no reason to feel superior.

If you notice you're wanting to feel superior, ask yourself what you lack that would be filled in by a sense of being dominant. What do you need that lording yourself over another would supply? Then, what do you need to do to fill the hole in yourself?

Judge Not . . . Really?

Some people say that none of us should judge at all, at any time. They believe that to judge is to be spiritually arrogant. If you subscribe to that point of view, you will fall into the very arrogance you are trying to avoid. For every attempt you make to be nonjudgmental, every time you say, perhaps with a chuckle to cover yourself, "I don't mean that as a judgment," your mind has already formulated the judgment or you would have no reason to proclaim against making it. So you are caught in both arrogance and hypocrisy.

You make judgments all the time. You prefer one car over another, one friend over another, one parent over the other. You cannot function without making judgments. Besides, when you say you should never judge, that's a judgment.

Yes, the Bible tells us, "Judge not, lest ye be judged." We would suggest that speaks more to contempt and condemnation than it does the observations, discernments, and evaluations we must make to function in our lives. So relax. Let yourself be human. That will keep you grounded in the reality of how you, as a brain/mind/self, actually organize your reactions to both inner and outer experience.

If, by not judging, you want to be kind and compassionate, then do so by all means. The world needs all the compassion and care you can bring. Even better, forgive and be forgiven. We all blunder. Accepting responsibility, welcoming accountability, and making amends is far more spiritually sound than trying not to be human.

Accepting Reality

There are skills that will help you to avoid the pitfalls:

- Stay present in the moment.

- Open to the reality of your situation.

- Remember that your partner is not you.

- Receive what is given you.

- Remember that conflict is a call for change.

- Practice being curious.

- Practice being kind.

- Keep romance alive.

Each of these is a basic element of living every day as a form of practical spirituality. Use them as reminders to actively enjoy the miracle of being together.

Exploring
The Grace of Deep Intimacy

1. Consciously watch your spouse as she is opening the mail, as he kisses the kids good-bye, as she gets ready for a special evening with you, as he mows the lawn. Take nothing for granted. Observe the way she holds her mouth, the way he tips his chin. Notice her intensity, his focus, her spirit, his passion. Watch as if this were the last time you'd see your beloved on earth. Notice what you feel and what you want to tell your lover about your experience. And then, as an expression of grace, give your spouse a full description of what you observed and felt.

2. Take turns making love to one another. Yes, *to*. Not with. The receiving partner can choose to be entirely passive and receptive or can choose to request whatever he or she desires. When you are receiving, hold in consciousness that your lover is a gift and so is the lovemaking that is to be received. Embrace this time of pure and total attention solely on you and your pleasure.

    When you are the giving partner, remember that you are a channel for grace. Your passionate love and your generous desire to please and provide pleasure are a divine expression of grace. Experience your lovemaking as an active prayer of enjoyment, gratitude, and humility.

3. While this won't work for everyone, it is a beautiful way of gracing one another. Imagine, if your spouse had passed away, what you would want to say for your eulogy. Write it all out.

    Share your eulogy with your spouse. Don't rush through it. Make sure you say everything you'd ever want to say. And don't just read it—look up and make eye contact. Feel the feelings of love and potential loss. Let these feelings come forward. Take nothing about your life together for granted. Share all the moments of rich grace.

And then celebrate with a wake or a feast for the blessing of still having one another, when you can both still revel in the grace of being with one another here on earth.

CHAPTER TWENTY

The Principles:
Surrender, Surrender, Surrender

The Grace of Deep Intimacy is not something you can feel every moment. But be assured, it is always present in support of your love. The seven principles below are not meant as rules or obligations, but as you practice them, grace will become more a part of your daily, conscious experience.

Stay Open to the Expansion of Your Life's Story

So often, even with fairly advanced awareness, you can still act from preconceived notions of how life is going to go, how a plan will unfold, how you imagine feeling when something special happens. We all live with expectations. That's part of being alive.

But when your expectations are unconscious, they drive much of how you behave. Why? Because they are beyond your awareness and your capacity to choose what you expect. As a result, you are limited by them. That blocks the larger, open-ended flow of possibilities and actually thwarts the spiritual adventure your soul wants you to pursue.

Remember how Jim's brother, Bill, met his wife by going to our relationship weekend that he'd not wanted to attend?

Remember how Nick and Barb had lived a few houses away from one another and never met until he answered her personals ad on the Internet?

Our nephew, Josh, was moving into his dorm room for his first year at college. Meagan, who lived on the floor above, came and asked if he and his roommate would help with a heavy carpet she and her roommate wanted to put down. Later, Josh and Meagan became friends, and then more than friends, and all because of a cumbersome carpet.

To assure yourself the widest and deepest experience of grace, open to the mystery. The unexpected is always right around the corner. Make it a habit to wait and see. One event leads to another and to another and . . . who knows what's going to happen . . . what's beyond your imagination . . . right around the corner . . . if you'll only keep going . . . then you'll be there . . . and you'll find out!

Playfulness Is Highly Spiritual

Grace is often portrayed with monastic religious figures in dark cassocks walking and praying in a walled-in garden. But there needs to be room for a much larger image of grace, one in which laughter and play and even silliness are valued.

In our book *Opening to Love 365 Days a Year*, we wrote about how having fun together is one of the underrated ways of keeping romance alive and thriving. You're never too old to feel like a kid again, abandoned and giddy with delight, in your own rollicking creativity. That quality of grace acts like Silly Putty, filling any gaps in your connection.

When you run into areas of conflict that aren't easily resolved, due to entrenched lifelong beliefs that don't readily yield to immediate change, you can find ways to ease the tension with humor. If it's a nervous habit, you can lovingly tease about it. Don't just suck it up and pretend everything's okay. It's not. But you can loosen up, and be cute and lovingly mischievous. Many things don't have to be *so* serious. They become far less problematic when you're free to kid about them.

Years ago a couple we knew, Maurizia and Michael, moved into an old house that needed a lot of work. She was the organizer. He was the laborer. We ran into them at a paint store and asked how it was going.

"It's a honeydew day," he said, laughing.

"Honeydew?" Jim asked.

"Sure," he pointed to Maurizia, "she smiles at me and says honey do this, honey do that." They both laughed, exchanging a knowing glance.

Their playful banter flowed easily from their warm, trusting humor. That's how they handled the sometimes awkward tension that arose from their roles as organizer and laborer. Their teasing turned into a form of real romance.

Natasha and Drew are the owners of The Country Store, a wonderful cafe and gift shop in our town. They work long hours to keep the store going.

Natasha teases about how Drew is such a baby when he's sick—all 6'5" of his handsome, lanky self. He just smiles that intimate smile of "yeah, and I love how you baby me!"

They share a zest for life and a casual freedom that you can feel in the grace between them.

In our relationship, the longer we're together the more silly, funny, and intimately teasing we've become. There's such grace in the merriment we share, in the deep knowing that our laughter is only available to us when we stop being so serious and open to the lighter side.

Bring It to Light—It Will Grace Your Love

There's never an end to getting to know one another. You have new experiences, you change. Life happens, you read about it in the paper or see it on the evening news, and you are changed. New responses. New awareness. New ways of being.

Some of them will be dark. Even devastating. A child's death. A false accusation that costs you your job. Your parents suddenly divorce after thirty-five years of marriage. Your world is rocked. Compassion is called for. As you share the shock and grief, the caretaking and endless details, compassion can bring a state of grace even at the worst of times.

A couple who attended one of our weekend trainings had been married for seven years when her youthful, active, beloved father was killed in an automobile accident. Her world crumbled. She was racked with grief, the extent to which surprised her. She'd also been the key take-charge person in her family of origin, so her siblings looked to her to be the strong one. She couldn't do that and felt shame and guilt for what she thought was weakness. Intellectually, she knew she wasn't failing, but emotionally she couldn't keep out the voices that chastised her for feeling overcome.

Her husband was filled with compassion for her. He was right at her side all the way. He took charge of the legal and business details. He held her when she wept and listened to her tell her favorite memories. He was her comfort, her strength, and her protector. His love graced both of them as he offered the harbor in which she could feel safe.

But this wasn't one-way love. As she surrendered to the full experience of losing her father, she also gave herself even more fully to her marriage. She included her husband in the depth of her grief, and their already strong bond was strengthened even further through the intimacy brought on by this death and the compassion needed to get through it.

Anytime you bring an issue out into the light of love, it can only bring you closer. The key is to stay open. The grace is there.

Be in the World but Not of It

You are in the world because you live on this planet. But you don't have to lose yourself and be possessed by it.

We received a request for help through the advice section of our online newsletter. The couple had been married for three years and were no longer able to ignore their clashing values. He was obsessed with what everyone thought of them—their house, their vacations, their artwork, everything. She wanted to focus on the quality of their life and what they were trying to build together.

He felt battered about, a pawn of the world. She made her living in it but had pulled back to look at living within her own purpose, her own vision. Watching his anxiety and how he always felt inadequate to meet his own expectations, she wanted a different vision for their relationship. Several months later she emailed again telling us of their impending divorce. He was unable to extricate himself from his obsession with what he believed others thought of him. He was of the world but, ironically, not really in it.

You can't worry about what others think of your relationship—whether it's where you live, how you choose your friends, what you each do to make your living, the values you choose in raising your children. Without a sense of yourself, you will get swallowed up. Your soul will be stifled under the pressures to fit in, to belong, to be "normal."

At the same time, you cannot reject the world, not even for so-called higher reasons. Even if you moved to a mountaintop and lived off the land, your choices would still be dictated by the world you were trying to flee.

Respecting life as the Creator fashioned it means living in the world, actively impacting it as it impacts you—a reciprocal relationship, giving and receiving. After all, the world is what you make of it. Or don't. If you cannot assert your presence, it will have its way with you. Not unlike what happens in any relationship. For there to be the presence of grace, there have to be two equal contributing partners. In the previous example, the man was so consumed by the world that he was its prisoner.

What's Right about This?

When things are looking bleak, out of balance, or just plain weird, to keep your vision open to the grace that may be appearing in an unfamiliar form, ask yourself, "What's right about this?"

There is always some wisdom trying to catch your attention. If you stay fixed in *should*s and *ought*s, or cling to an image or idea that you've already developed, you will miss what may be right in front of you because the message is coming from beyond what you've imagined.

Our friends Sharon Smiley and Brad Lusk have been together nine years, married five. When they met they were both struggling with stressful and unsatisfying careers. The situation challenged their health, their sanity, and the development of their relationship.

They each had issues about money. Brad felt obligated to provide for both of them, which kept him feeling trapped in a career in radio management that had become stale and routine. Sharon, who worked as a motivational sales trainer for a large cosmetics company, had been forced to carry the entire financial responsibility in a previous marriage and now she feared that if Brad changed careers or became unemployed, she would have to bear that burden again.

But life had its own plan.

With little warning, Brad was forced out of his twenty-year career. They were both frightened by the uncertainty of Brad's future, and Sharon's panic overwhelmed her.

Old demons dominated Sharon's reluctance to shoulder their bills, while guilty defensiveness perpetually showed up in Brad's daily thoughts and his attitude toward Sharon. They were worried that their marriage would not survive the crisis.

Then one night over dinner they took a long look at what was right about their situation. They affirmed the blessing of having met at a party neither had wanted to attend. They confirmed that they loved each other deeply. And they reminded themselves that they had married with the understanding that they were committed to their own and one another's personal growth.

From there it became easier to see that Brad's job loss was the right thing to have happened. Only that way could he reinvent himself in a career that would be inspiring and creative.

They cut back their lifestyle to ease the burden on Sharon while Brad started his new life as a self-employed clinical exercise and health specialist for seniors. At the same time it was agreed that as soon as Brad's new career could support them, Sharon would quit her job and pursue her dreams. They were sure that it was all going to be quite all right.

Today Brad is their very enthusiastic breadwinner while Sharon completes her education in counseling.

It really was all right—right from the beginning!

Our experience with clients, friends, and in our own relationship has proven that asking "What's right about this?" is one of the wisest responses we can have during a befuddling, even painful time. It reaffirms faith in a Higher Order trust that something good will inevitably come, and it invites our souls to speak to us more clearly. It keeps us on the track of adventure and discovery, so that fear and depression are less likely to take over. It grounds us in the here and now, rather than in worry and anxiety based on ungrounded fantasies of the future. And it steadies our openness to curiosity, which always makes room for grace to respond.

Do unto Others . . . What They Want

The Golden Rule says: "Do unto others as you would have them do unto you." But that assumes everyone is just like you.

We propose a new Golden Rule that reads: "Do unto others as they would like you to do unto them." With the caveat, "When in doubt, ask."

Remember our friends Laurie and Denny? When they were not feeling well, they did precisely unto each other what they would want done to them. She babied him because that's what she wanted. He left her alone because that's what he wanted. Neither one took the time to find out what the other wanted. They were caught in the *old* Golden Rule, which resulted in a form of naive narcissism and it led them to divorce court.

But when they took the time to ask and find out what each other wanted, they learned to do unto each other what each other wanted done unto them. They have lived by that principle ever since they remarried, and now delight in pleasuring each other in ways that are inclusive and very meaningful.

You open to grace only when you are offering your love, your care, your compassion in a way that speaks to the person receiving it. And your sincere curiosity is a grace in itself.

Give Yourself Completely to Love

Surrender, surrender, surrender to love. Give yourself completely to what love wants from you and perhaps, more important, what your soul wants *for* you. When you do, you will find yourself living from the center of your heart.

When you give yourself to the power of love, you can pull out all the stops. Abandon inhibitions. Jettison fears. Express your passions. Melt into the connection with the one you love. Allow love to take you where you've never been—with each other as well as in the world. Then the power of love will redeem you into grace, again and again and again.

Exploring
The Grace of Deep Intimacy

1. Enjoy the grace of making love out of bed. Here's one way to do it.

   Sit on a couch, the largest of you with your back to the couch, feet on the ground. The smaller of you sits facing the back of the couch, legs drawn up onto the couch and your hips touching. (As a teenager, you may have found this combination really comfy for "necking," "fooling around," or whatever the expression was when you were that age.)

   Put your arms around one another, look directly into each other's eyes, and *make love out of bed*. The goal is not sexual per se, but sensual, emotional, and passionately spiritual. Take your time exploring, talking, kissing. Feel the pleasure of just blending your bodies into one another.

Speak all that you feel, everything you think, even what you've never thought of saying. Allow the deep grace between you to express in every way possible. And receive, receive, receive what is given to you by your beloved and what wells up from within. Allow grace to emerge between you. Trust that you are safe, and go where you've never gone before.

2. For an afternoon or even a full day, take turns having playdates. One of you will be the designated five-year-old. The other the loving, playful adult. The five-year-old can request, in advance or during the day, any kind of activity he or she might desire. It's up to the "adult" to plan the day, drive, escort the "kid," and pay for everything. The kid gets completely taken care of and just plays and plays and plays!

Think in terms of activities you loved as a child or never got to do—flying kites, blowing bubbles, being pushed on a swing, face painting, horseback riding, or scary stuff kids love like flying in a glider, going on a roller coaster or Ferris wheel, or milder stuff like the merry-go-round or bumper cars. You might include kid places like the children's museum or a children's movie. And make sure you eat a lot. Kids love to go to restaurants that have crayons on the table and paper covers to draw on. They love ice cream and cake. And they love to laugh and roll down hills at the park.

The point is for both of you to have a time of pure fun and for one of you to be in the full protection and loving care of the other.

3. When both of you have finished reading this book, create a remarriage ceremony for just the two of you. Write your own

vows, either separately or together. Give thought to what you say to one another, for you are designing the template of your future together. Decide on any readings or prayers you would both like included. You may want music in the background, candlelight, and flowers. You may even want to set up your videorecorder to capture your remarriage, to add to your special collection of photo or video memories.

Create a special evening for your ceremony and invite grace to be with you by giving your heart and soul to all that you say and all that you receive. Then celebrate yourselves with a wonderful dinner out or anything else you would both especially enjoy.

CHAPTER TWENTY-ONE

The Payoff:
Let Me Come to You

*T*he Gates of Eden are open to you once again. This time you have earned the right to be there. Not as an obedient child, but as a conscious and maturing expression of love. The Fiery Angel no longer forbids you entry.

The Garden is the miracle of your everyday life, and beauty is all around and within you. Not only are the roses beautiful, but now you also know the beauty of the thorns, the weeds, and even the worms in the sod. The mundane is sacred and the sacred is mundane. You live with gratitude, rejoicing at being able to share it with the one who has become your soul mate. Through trial by fire and the alchemical magic of your differences, your relationship has become an expression of everyday grace.

Three Have Become as One

At the outset of the First Passage, two strangers met and were attracted. As you crossed through, you merged together emotionally, sexually, spiritually. You knew you were made for one another. The experience was exquisite and two became as one.

For your love to succeed, the Second Passage took you into the fire. The oneness receded as you distinguished yourselves as separate individuals, each with a point of view that had to be recognized and valued. It was then that one became two again.

During the Third Passage, as you lived from your understanding that the other person was not you, you opened to, explored, and cherished the differences between you. Your respect and admiration deepened as you discovered the extent to which there was wisdom in your choice. The two of you, joined by your love, together gave birth to your relationship. In that way, two became three.

In the Fourth Passage you are secure in yourselves. You completely trust your being together. Your faith is abundant and you are graced by the transcendent. God, meaning that which is the core, the fountain, the intimacy, the beginning and end of all that is, permeates your consciousness. You live connected with all of life. So now, what was three is again as one.

That oneness is the spiritual miracle of this life, and it has been with you from the first moment.

Love Does Make the World Go 'Round

You now know that love isn't just a sweet feeling or a sentimental desire. It really is the stuff that passes all understanding, a power that can indeed move mountains. More important, it is the urge through which you and your beloved unite.

Moving Mountains

You've seen it in yourself when, against all odds, you claimed that metaphoric height, the goal that seemed insurmountable. With the force of love supporting you, you gave your all. You earned that degree, lost that weight, beat that cancer, or made your marriage work when everyone said it couldn't be done. You moved those mountains of fear, filled in the valleys of submission. You let go of your old identity to make room for the new. You knew all it took was the unyielding belief that it could be done and the two of you committed to making it happen. It was love seeing you through. That's the power of the love you share.

Your Internal Observer

Practiced in the ways of self-awareness, you become aware of a kind of soul conscience, your internal observer and guide who is always asking the question for you, "Are you coming from love?"

The term *making love* is most often used to apply to sex, seldom to our interactions with others. Now, in your *Grace of Deep Intimacy,* you can rely on your conscience to make certain you are making love in the ways you relate with the outer world.

Love wants to love everything. And now, through your evolved capacity for love, your observing self-awareness helps you serve the desires of love.

Personal Liberation

When you've learned to stand solidly in your own identity, in the world but not of it, you are secure for life. Fear no longer shadows your consciousness. You know without wavering that your relationship will last your lifetime.

The key to that liberation is your total commitment to the love you share and your full commitment to helping one another live nothing less than full lives. Like falling asleep or releasing yourself to an orgasm, liberation comes only when you surrender—giving yourself over to your soul's call—over and over again.

Wonder and Joy

When you've attained *The Grace of Deep Intimacy,* you have moved into an intimacy with all of life, an enlightenment that opens you to live the joy and wonder that is present for you every day. During the First Passage you tasted it, but you were not ready to live it daily. Now you are.

There is a parallel between love in the Fourth Passage and what this Zen proverb points to: Before enlightenment, chop wood, carry water. After enlightenment, chop wood, carry water.

In the beginning when you chopped wood and carried the water, it felt like a job. That's how many couples feel about what they encounter in the Second Passage. "Love shouldn't be this much work," they cry.

But now, in the Fourth Passage, your awareness has matured so that the details of living your love are not a burden but a welcome expression of the life you have co-created. Following the Zen imagery, you now chop wood and are grateful that it heats your home and can be used to build your new bathroom and make baseball bats and embroidery hoops. As you carry water, you give thanks for the thirst-quenching miracle supplied every day, and you are reminded of how much you love a hot shower and how your garden thrives when you water it regularly.

Wood and water are metaphors for everything in life. When you are undeveloped you lack appreciation, you lack consciousness of the miracle of life. But by the Fourth Passage you know that everything in life is meaningful, everything in life is either a cause for celebration or a cause for new learning.

The beauty of the arc of love is that it not only produces the relationship you've dreamed of, but it also grows you into the mature magnificence you are meant to be. And it continually opens your awareness to seeing the one you love and all of life with wonder and joy.

It is this sacred connection with all of life that transforms your daily life into a sacrament, a walking prayer.

Everything Is Romantic

Filled with love—the love of your spouse, the love you give yourself, and the abundance of your everyday life—generosity is now an everyday habit. You extend kindness and care to one another and receive each other to complete the circle. It is all romantic.

You take yourselves into the outer world and beam spiritual generosity on those you encounter. You are a radiance of love. And it is romantic.

The work you do for a living is no longer arduous. Rather, it is an expression of your character. Your work has now become a creative pleasure. It is a way you can offer your love and generosity to the world at large, a form of practical romance.

You are best friends who love to be together, trusted allies in good times and bad.

Your life together is the creation of your shared expression, separately and together, and because of that, everything you do is romantic.

Your Love Life Is a Paradigm for the Whole of Your Life

What you have learned and continue to learn about love is also a model for parenting, careers, and the rest of your life.

When you practice respecting differences by remembering that the other person is not you, be it your child or your boss, and you hold the well-being of the relationship as your priority, you can put forth what you need in a way that is straightforward and respectful. You won't always get what you want, but the dialogue is open, and then who knows what's possible.

"Well, I can't do that with my kids," you're protesting. "They need to be given rules. And my boss, am I supposed to get into a fight with her?" Those are longstanding attitudes, to be sure, but they distance you from your children and your life.

For example, if you learn that your child won't listen to you, you have succeeded in discovering that there are deeper issues. Rather than trying to force your will upon your child, you can shift your focus to what is truly at the source of his or her resistance. Then at least you will be dealing with what is actually going on, rather than misfiring and frustrating everyone involved.

If your boss isn't open to dialogue, there's nothing you can do. But you will certainly know the responsibility is not yours. If it's not possible to leave, you can decide how to respond from a perspective grounded in reality. Then you can focus on taking care of yourself rather than being at the mercy of his or her reactions.

When others criticize you, it's only their side you're hearing. You can receive what they say with conscious curiosity and not have to take it personally. You know to leave the space open for dialogue so you can better understand what is intended.

With a minority of people, dialogue will not be possible, no matter how available, loving, and kind you may be. They will be so emotionally limited that they will not be able to grant you your separate otherness. If that is the case, you may choose to walk away and close the door, since any true relating is impossible. It's only through negotiating mutually desirable outcomes that you can achieve a loving, grace-filled life.

Serial Monogamy with the Same Person

As you reach *The Grace of Deep Intimacy,* you continue to enjoy what we call *serial monogamy with the same person.* In other words, you continue to have different relationships—with your spouse.

The end of any phase of your life together is never a need to leave, but an invitation to the next relationship the two of you will create. It may mean starting your own business, traveling, moving to your dream house, developing a new health and exercise regime, writing a book about your life together—for your kids or for publication. The sky's the limit when you know you can continually reinvent your love and life together.

Rather than a midlife crisis taking you out of the house for a fling, you create that new fling with your spouse. Rather than the empty-nest syndrome taking you into someone else's arms for comfort and support, you discover that new support and wondrous comfort with your spouse. And retirement can become a time of new romance, new adventure. As we all continue to live longer, this aspect of romantic consciousness becomes even more important.

Serial monogamy with the same person celebrates the opportunity to regenerate your life, your love, and your sexual passion. It honors the rich complexity of each of you and guarantees you'll never be bored and never take each other for granted.

Sacred Sex

The art of sacred sex lives in the miracle of your desire to make of your bodies a testament to pleasure and to move beyond all that separates you. And you are open to receive the blessing of this communion in the name of all that is sacred to you.

In ordinary consciousness you use your bodies to define where each of you exists and you use your skin as the obvious enclosure of your private space. In *The Grace of Deep Intimacy,* your bodies, your skin, your senses become sacred vehicles of transcendence. You are an expression of an un-self-conscious passion. There is no goal but to surrender to that oneness in which you and your spouse are whole as distinct persons while being, at the same time, surrendered to your union that is the source of your wholeness. Three have become as one.

You may find yourself weeping, spellbound in awe. You may find surrender and resurrection into wholeness through sexual connection to be overwhelming at first. And yet you return to taste the grace of your sexuality as prayer, as gratitude, as the culmination of all that you have learned through love.

The Last Passage

We are mortal. This life ends. Death is the transition to . . . what? No one knows. However, as you trust the inherent wisdom of life you can look to your experience, because the Source of life may have provided clues there for what is to come.

Can you conceive of a pure ending, nothing at all hereafter? Is there any evidence in your experience for that possibility?

Well, when you resist what life brings to you—allowing fear and negativity to dominate—you become constricted and depressed and your life slows down. You may even feel that things have come to an end because there's nothing to look forward to. There is a connection between resistance and a sense of nothingness. That's not an unfamiliar experience and it is embedded deep in the fabric of this life.

But when you are open, you come to know that in every ending there is a beginning. You pass through who you are into a time of transition and then you move on to what you've never been before. So there is a connection between your open-hearted willingness and life going on. That process too is embedded deep in the very fabric of this life.

When you surrender to discovery and change as a way of expressing love, you care enough to carry on. You let go of what no longer works and you take on what life brings to you, knowing you are supported in your grand adventure.

So there is choice. Sometimes limited, sometimes expansive. This life is yours to do with as you will. You can resist or you can choose to be open.

Then, at the threshold of the last passage—that ultimate mystery of this life—your arms will be either folded or wide. By the way you love, perhaps you will have chosen what is next.

Our Wish for You

Let the love that lives between you intoxicate you with the miracle of who you are. Open to the goodness that exists in each of you, no matter what form or shape it may take. Leave room in your heart to embrace the darker side as well. Surrender to the force that moves you to care, to feel compassion, to speak over and over that the one you love is so very, very special. And then grace whispers . . .

Let me come to you and I will.

Sometimes I will visit you when you least expect it.

Other times, you may feel me right around the corner.

And at still other times, we will be one.

Let me come to you and I will come more and more and more.

I may come to you when you tuck your little one into bed or even when you're taking out the trash.

I may find you when you're saying good-bye to your dying mother, and bring you the peace you've both so sorely missed.

I may even find you when you're feeling lost and so alone, only to remind you that there is so much more going on in this life than you will ever be aware.

And I certainly will be there when you are dancing, your heart radiating life and love.

Let me come to you.

About the Authors

Judith Sherven, Ph.D. and **James Sniechowski, Ph.D.,** husband-and-wife psychology team, are authors of the breakthrough bestseller *The New Intimacy: Discovering the Magic at the Heart of Your Differences* (HCI) and *Opening to Love 365 Days a Year* (HCI).

Two of the country's most respected and pioneering authorities, Judith & Jim are revolutionizing the understanding of differences in relationships. Judith, a clinical psychologist, has worked with thousands of men and women in her twenty-two years of private practice. Jim holds a doctorate in Human Behavior and is the founder of The Menswork Center and cofounder of The Men's Health Network in Washington, D.C.

They have worked with close to 100,000 singles and couples in their relationship trainings, workshops, seminars, and lectures, as well as corporate consultations, nationally and overseas. They have appeared on over 600 radio and television shows including *Oprah, The View, New Attitudes, CNN, 48 Hours, MSNBC News with Brian Williams, Mars & Venus, The O'Reilly Factor, Leeza,* and *This Evening with Judith Regan.* They have a three-hour online call-in talk show on Wisdom Radio, and a weekly ezine that reaches over 50,000 people in over 100 countries.

Judith & Jim have written for or been interviewed by the *Los Angeles Times, Chicago Tribune, San Francisco Chronicle, London Sunday Times, Wall Street Journal, USA Today, Redbook, Essence, Glamour, First for Women, Black Elegance, Playboy, Modern Bride, Parents' Magazine, Black Men, Belle,* and *Family Circle.* They write regular columns for *Today's Black Woman* and *The Looking Glass.*

They live in a 200-year-old farmhouse in upstate New York, and have been married for fourteen years.

For More Information about Judith & Jim

You can visit their Web page at www.thenewintimacy.com.

You can enjoy their free weekly email newsletter by sending a blank email to join-thenewintimacy@lists.sparklist.com.

And you can listen to their show Saturdays on Wisdom Radio at www.wisdomradio.com.